ENGLISH
At Your Command!

Practice Book

D1358663

HAMPTON-BROWN

Table of Contents

Color, Size, and Shape Words

📖 Use Handbook pages 12–13.

- Look at the objects in your classroom, at school, or at home.

- Write sentences to tell about their colors, sizes, and shapes.

1. 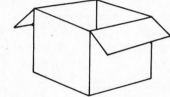 *The basketball is round. It is orange and black.* _____

2.  _____

3.  _____

4.  _____

5. _____

6. _____

Number Words

📖 Use Handbook page 14.

- Draw a picture of something that has a number on it.
- Use number words to write the number.

1.

one thousand nine hundred ninety-nine

4.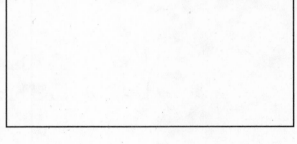

_____

2.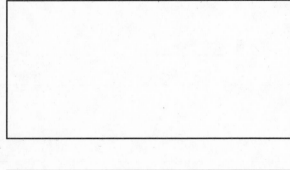

_____

5.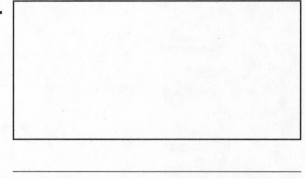

_____

3.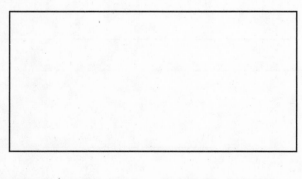

_____

6.

_____

Order Words/More Words
That Tell How Many

📖 Use Handbook page 15.

- **Read the story.**

- **Write a word from the box to finish each sentence.**

On June ____fourth____
1

my family had a big birthday

party to celebrate everyone's

birthday at the same time.

My grandmother had her _____ birthday in
2

February. We gave her a _____ of purple slippers.
3

Aunt Marta turned forty on the eighth of April. It was her

_____ birthday. We gave her _____
4   5

of books. Uncle Robert's birthday was a _____
6

days after Aunt Marta's. He got a new golf club and

_____ golf balls.
7

At the party, we sang "Happy Birthday" _____
8

times and played games. Before everyone left, we agreed to

celebrate again next year.

fortieth
pair
seventieth
some
few
several
fourth
a lot

Sensory Words

📖 Use Handbook pages 16–17.

- Draw a picture of your favorite meal.

- Write sentences to tell how each food looks, feels, smells, sounds, and tastes.

```

```

_____

_____

_____

_____

_____

_____

_____

Feeling Words

📖 Use Handbook page 18.

■ Read the feeling word.

■ Write a sentence about a time you felt that way.

1. angry   *I was angry when my toy spaceship*
   fell apart. _____ .

2. bored   _____
               _____ .

3. sad   _____
               _____ .

4. happy   _____
               _____ .

5. puzzled   _____
               _____ .

6. surprised   _____
               _____ .

7. embarrassed _____
               _____ .

8. afraid   _____
               _____ .

■ Now tell about two other feelings you have had.

9. I felt _____ when _____
   _____ .

10. I felt _____ when _____
    _____ .

Words That Tell Where

📖 **Use Handbook page 19.**

- **Look at the picture.**
- **Choose a word from the box to finish each sentence. Tell about the picture.**

1. The soccer ball is in _____*front of*_____ the net.

2. The ball is _____ the ground.

3. The ball is _____ Players 1 and 3.

4. Player 1 is _____ the bench.

5. A pair of shoes is _____ the bench.

6. There is a hat _____ the bag.

7. A big water bottle is _____ the bench.

8. Player 2 is _____ the bench.

far away from
behind
between
front of
inside
next to
on
under

Multiple-Meaning Words

📖 Use Handbook pages 21–24.

■ **Name each picture. Write the part of speech for the word.**

■ **Then write a sentence about the picture using the multiple-meaning word.**

1. 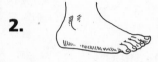 bat, noun   I hit a home run with my new baseball bat.

2.  _____   _____

3. _____   _____

4.  _____   _____

5. _____   _____

6.  _____   _____

7. _____   _____

8.  _____   _____

Multiple-Meaning Words

📖 Use Handbook pages 24–26.

- Read each sentence.
- Find the correct meaning of the word in dark print. Fill in the circle for the answer.

1. Last year I **left** Vietnam and came to my new school.
 ● to go away from ○ opposite of right ○ remaining

2. My teacher was **Miss** Adams.
 ○ to long for ○ an unmarried woman ○ to not hit a target

3. She asked me to **point** to my home country on the map.
 ○ to show ○ a dot on a line ○ a statement

4. Then she drew a **ring** around it with a red pen.
 ○ a circle ○ jewelry for the finger ○ the sound of a bell

5. Next, I showed the class my special **ring**.
 ○ the sound of a bell ○ jewelry for the finger ○ a circle

6. I always wear it on my **left** hand.
 ○ to go away from ○ opposite of right ○ remaining

7. When the bell began to **ring** we went out to play jump rope.
 ○ a circle ○ the sound of a bell ○ jewelry for the finger

8. I **miss** my friends in Vietnam, but I love my new home and school.
 ○ an unmarried woman ○ to not hit a target ○ to long for

Similes

📖 **Use Handbook page 28.**

- ■ **Look at the two pictures. Read the question.**
- ■ **Write the answer. Use a simile.**

Mr. Ruiz | ice

1. What are Mr. Ruiz's hands as cold as?

Mr. Ruiz's hands are
as cold as ice.

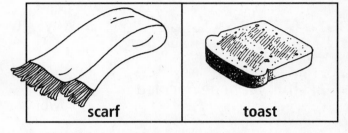

scarf | toast

4. What is the scarf as warm as?

_____

_____

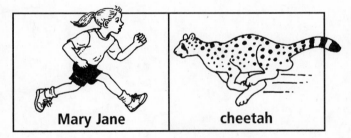

Mary Jane | cheetah

2. How does Mary Jane run?

_____

_____

Jake | kangaroo

5. How does Jake jump?

_____

_____

Mrs. Smith | bird

3. How does Mrs. Smith sing?

_____

_____

Tony | ox

6. What is Tony as strong as?

_____

_____

Sound-Alike Words

📖 Use Handbook pages 30–32.

- **Read each sentence.**

- **Choose the correct word below the line.
  Write the word in the blank.**

1. Antonio's ____aunt____ always gives him a special gift for his birthday.
   aunt/ant

2. This year she decided to _____ him concert tickets.
   by/buy

3. She bought _____ tickets so he could invite some friends.
   four/for

4. The tickets were _____ seats by the stage.
   four/for

5. Antonio was going to _____ his favorite band!
   see/sea

6. The show would start at _____ o'clock.
   ate/eight

7. They would leave after they _____ dinner.
   ate/eight

8. It would take an _____ to drive to the amphitheater.
   hour/our

9. The amphitheater was _____ the airport.
   by/buy

10. Antonio couldn't wait for the concert day to get _____!
    hear/here

Synonyms

📖 **Use Handbook pages 33–35.**

How to Play
The Synonym Game

1. Play with a partner.

2. Use an eraser or other small object as your game piece. Use a coin to show how many spaces to move.

    Heads = 1 space

   🪙 Tails = 2 spaces

3. Say the word in the space.

4. Say a synonym for the word. Then use the synonym in a sentence. For example: *cold–freezing. It's **freezing** outside.*

5. The first one to reach **THE END** wins.

Board spaces: BEGIN, cold, eat, like, bad, mad, laugh, go, little, noisy, afraid, happy, good, big, brave, cry, THE END

Synonyms

Use Handbook pages 33–37.

■ **Read the paragraph. Look at the underlined words.**

■ **Rewrite the paragraph. Replace the underlined words with synonyms.**

I <u>like</u> soccer! Last night my mom and I went to a soccer match. I was <u>happy</u> to be there. It was <u>cold</u> outside. So I got a <u>warm</u> drink. I <u>ate</u> a hamburger, too. The Seahawks were playing well. All their players are <u>strong</u>. When they <u>go</u> down the field no one can stop them. When the Seahawks scored the first goal, the crowd started to <u>talk</u>. The cheering was <u>noisy</u>. It started to rain, but it was such a <u>good</u> game that no one wanted to go home until the end!

I love soccer! _____

_____

_____

_____

_____

_____

_____

_____

_____

_____

_____

_____

Antonyms

📖 Use Handbook pages 38–39.

- Write a word from Handbook pages 38–39 in the box. Then write a sentence using the word.

- Ask your partner to write the antonym for the word and write a sentence using the antonym.

1. _____ clean _____ My shirt is clean. _____ _____	_____ dirty _____ My shirt is dirty. _____ _____
2. _____ _____ _____	_____ _____ _____
3. _____ _____ _____	_____ _____ _____
4. _____ _____ _____	_____ _____ _____
5. _____ _____ _____	_____ _____ _____
6. _____ _____ _____	_____ _____ _____

Time and Measurement

📖 Use Handbook pages 40–41.

■ **Read the questions.**

■ **Write the answers. Use time words.**

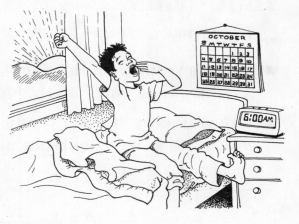

1. When do you wake up?

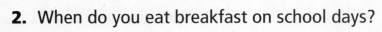 _I wake up at 6:00 a.m. daily._ _____

2. When do you eat breakfast on school days?

_____

3. When do you leave for school?

_____

4. When do you eat lunch?

_____

5. When do you get home from school?

_____

6. When do you do your homework?

_____

7. When do you have dinner?

_____

8. When do you go to bed?

_____

9. What do you do on Saturdays?

_____

10. What is your favorite time of day?

_____

Time and Measurement

📖 Use Handbook page 43.

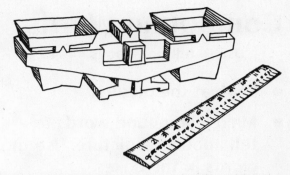

- Use a ruler or a scale to measure or weigh six things in the classroom.

- Complete the chart.

What I Measured or Weighed	What I Learned About It
1. my English book	It is 8 inches wide and 10 inches long. It weighs 1 pound, 7 ounces.
2.	
3.	
4.	
5.	
6.	

Compound Words

📖 Use Handbook pages 44–45.

- Look at the picture.

- Make compound words to tell about the picture. Use the words in the boxes.

1. *summertime*

2. _____

3. _____

4. _____

5. _____

First Part	+	Second Part
summer		shine
out		noon
back		time
sun		side
after		yard

6. _____

7. _____

8. _____

9. _____

10. _____

First Part	+	Second Part
lunch		burgers
table		apple
ham		time
water		melon
pine		cloth

Suffixes

📖 Use Handbook pages 46–47.

■ Read each sentence.

■ Find the suffix that can be added to the word. Fill in the circle for the answer. Then write the word with the suffix.

1. Jackie is a **paint**___.
   ● -er   ○ -ward   ○ -en

_____painter_____

2. She paints **wood**___ masks.
   ○ -ward   ○ -er   ○ -en

_____

3. She has to be very neat and **care**___.
   ○ -ible   ○ -ful   ○ -less

_____

4. Jackie has a cat that is very **play**___.
   ○ -en   ○ -ward   ○ -ful

_____

5. Once, the cat knocked a paint can over **back**___.
   ○ -er   ○ -ible   ○ -ward

_____

6. Thank goodness the paint wasn't **break**___ !
   ○ -en   ○ -able   ○ -ful

_____

7. Jackie cleaned up the **harm**___ puddle of paint.
   ○ -ible   ○ -en   ○ -less

_____

8. Jackie only uses paints that are **wash**___ !
   ○ -able   ○ -ward   ○ -less

_____

Prefixes

 **Use Handbook pages 48–49.**

- **Read each sentence.**

- **Use a word with a prefix to replace the meaning below the blank.**

- **Write the word with the prefix.**

1. My sister and I like to ride our ____bicycles____ .
two-wheeled cycles

2. Riding is lots of fun, and it is _____ .
not expensive

3. We _____ riding on the streets, so we ride in the park.
don't like

4. Last weekend we _____ a ride with some friends.
plan before

5. Dad drove us to the park in our _____ .
small van

6. We rode back and forth in a _____ on the path.
half circle

7. Once, my water bottle fell off and I had to _____ it.
attach again

8. Dad used his new _____ to take pictures of us to send
small camera
to our grandparents.

Idioms

📖 Use Handbook pages 50–52.

- Work with a partner.

- Look at each picture. Write words from the box to finish what the girls are saying.

1.

Give it your best shot!	I'm all thumbs!
I've got cold feet.	Break a leg!

I can't go out there! _____
_____
_____
_____

Don't worry. _____
_____
_____

2.

That was as easy as pie.	I was as cool as a cucumber.
Now, pat yourself on the back!	I said it would be a piece of cake.

Wow! I did it. _____
_____
_____

I knew you could do it.
_____
_____
_____

Idioms

📖 Use Handbook pages 52–53.

- **Work with a partner.**

- **Finish what the boys are saying. Use words from the boxes.**

1.

| lend you a hand | in a jam | upside down | keep your shirt on |

I'm _in a jam_. I can't find my baseball card to trade. I've turned the room _____!

I'll _____.
Just _____!

2.

| You bet | pat ourselves on the back | put our heads together | off the hook |

I found it!
I'm _____.
When we _____
_____, we can do anything!

_____ we can.
We should _____
_____.

Two-Word Verbs

📖 **Use Handbook pages 54–55.**

■ **Read each sentence. Look at the verb in dark print.**

■ **Choose the correct word below the line to make a two-word verb. Write the word in the blank.**

1. We heard something **breaking**

   _____*up*_____ inside our car's
   out/up

   engine on Saturday.

2. Then the car **broke** _____, and
   down/up

   Dad and I had to walk everywhere.

3. First, we **checked** _____ on
   off/up

   Grandma to see if she was okay.

4. At Grandma's, we phoned Mom to **check** _____ with her.
   off/in

5. She **brought** _____ ideas for places to go like the library and the store.
   off/up

6. At the library, I **filled** _____ a form for a library card.
   off/out

7. At the store, Dad **brought** _____ the grocery list.
   out/on

8. We **checked** _____ everything on the list, and then carried
   up/off

   the groceries home.

Two-Word Verbs

📖 **Use Handbook pages 56–57.**

■ **Look at each picture. Read the sentence.**

■ **Write a two-word verb from the box in the blank.**

get over	give up	go away
get out	look over	give back

1. I hope I ___*get over*___ this cold soon.

2. I always _____ my homework before I turn it in.

3. I have to _____ my library book.

4. I want the rain to _____ so I can play outside.

5. I _____ of the bus at the corner near my house.

6. I won't _____ until I make ten baskets!

Two-Word Verbs

 Use Handbook pages 54–59.

■ **Read the story.**

■ **Write a two-word verb from the box in each blank.**

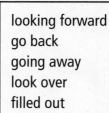

Maria is ____*going away*____ for a week
                    1

to Space Camp. She has been _____
                                          2

to this for a long time. Marc went last year and said it was

so much fun he wanted to _____ there.
                                    3

Last winter, Maria _____ an application.
                              4

The camp sent her lots of information to _____.
                                                    5

looking forward
go back
going away
look over
filled out

Yesterday, Maria packed. She _____ just
                                        6

the right clothes to wear. She carefully _____
                                                    7

each item from a list that the camp sent her.

Maria has to _____ at the camp very early
                    8

Monday morning. So she _____ the light
                                    9

and gets into bed. Maria can't go to sleep, though. She keeps

_____ and over because she's so excited
        10

about her trip!

check in
turns off
picked out
turning over
checked off

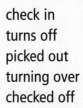

Character Map

📖 Use Handbook page 62.

■ **Think about a character from a story you've read.**

■ **Make a character map to show what that character is like.**

■ **Now cover up the name of your character and show the character map to a partner. Can your partner guess who the character is?**

Picture It!

Main Idea Cluster

📖 Use Handbook page 64.

- Think about an animal you know a lot about.

- Use what you know to finish the cluster. Write one sentence that tells the main idea about your animal. Then write details that tell more about the main idea.

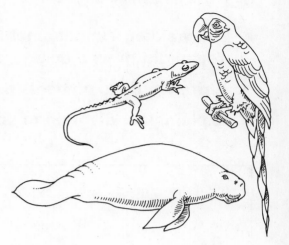

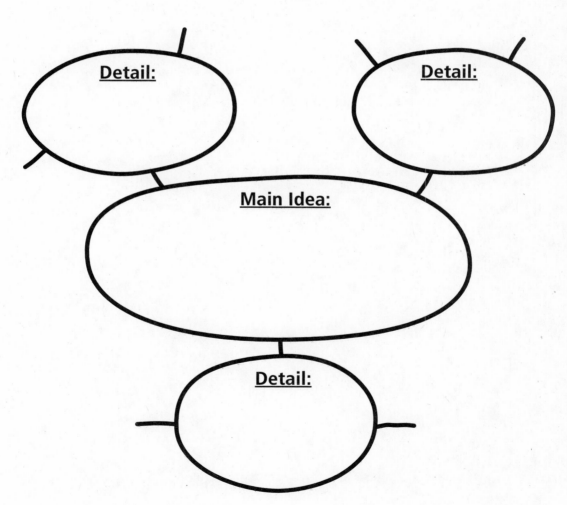

Parts Diagram

📖 **Use Handbook page 66.**

- **Draw a diagram of something that has lots of parts. You might draw a bicycle, a car, or a new invention!**

- **Write words to name its parts.**

- **Explain your diagram to your partner.**

Main Idea Diagram

📖 Use Handbook page 67.

- What special holiday or event does your family celebrate? Write a sentence about the holiday in the **Main Idea** box.

- Then write a sentence in each **Detail** box to tell what you do to get ready for the holiday.

Detail:

+

Detail:

+

Detail:

=

Main Idea:

Bar Graph

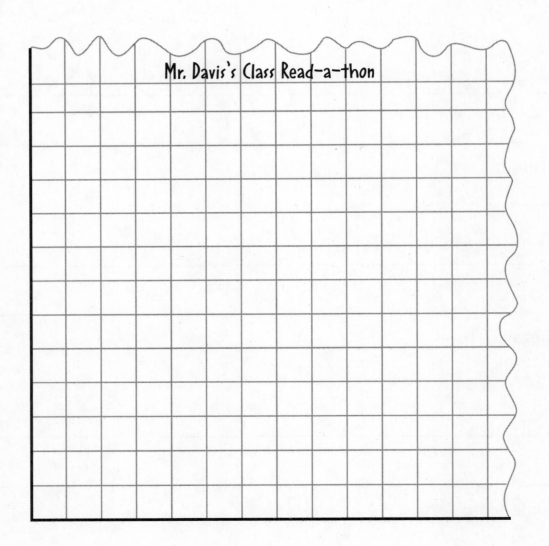

Use Handbook page 68.

- Read the information in the box.
- Use the information to make a bar graph.

Mr. Davis's Class Read-a-thon

Janell read 10 books.
Jin Ki read 7 books.
Hector read 12 books.
Claire read 6 books.

Mr. Davis's Class Read-a-thon

Pie Graph

📖 Use Handbook page 69.

- ■ Look at the pie graph.
- ■ Read each question.
- ■ Write the answer. Use complete sentences.

Popcorn Sold by Classes at Culver School

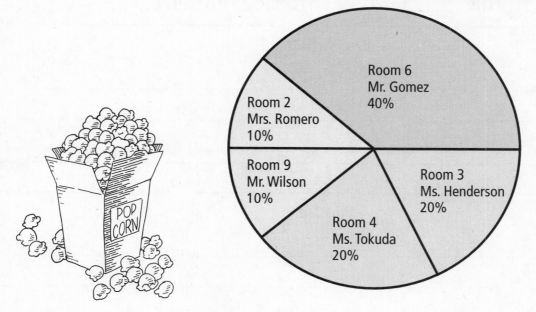

1. What percentage of popcorn did Mr. Gomez's class sell?

   _____

2. How do you know that Room 2 sold less than Room 4?

   _____

3. What percentage of popcorn did Ms. Henderson's class sell?

   _____

4. Did Mrs. Romero's class sell more than Mr. Wilson's?

   _____

5. Which class sold the most popcorn?

   _____

Beginning, Middle, and End Story Map

📖 Use Handbook page 71.

■ Read the story on Handbook page 141.

■ Finish the story map. Tell what happens in each part of the story.

Title: _Another Saturday Morning_

Beginning

_____

_____

⬇

Middle

1. _____

_____

2. _____

_____

3. _____

_____

4. _____

_____

⬇

End

_____

_____

_____

Name _____ Date _____

Story Staircase Map

📖 Use Handbook pages 76–77.

■ Work with a partner.

■ Read the fable on Handbook page 105.

■ Finish the story map to tell what happened.

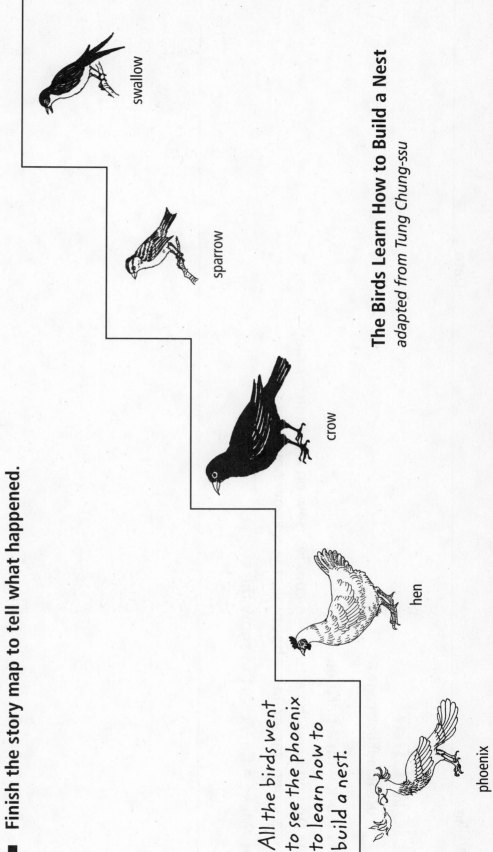

swallow

sparrow

crow

hen

phoenix

All the birds went
to see the phoenix
to learn how to
build a nest.

The Birds Learn How to Build a Nest
adapted from Tung Chung-ssu

Name _____ Date _____

Flow Chart

📖 Use Handbook page 81.

■ Work with a partner.

■ Do you know how to make cookies, sew on a button, or play a video game? Talk about what you know how to do.

■ Make a flow chart to show the steps.

Time Line

📖 **Use Handbook pages 82–83.**

■ **Think about important events in your life.**

■ **Tell about the events on the time line. Use ages or dates to show when the events happened.**

Name: _____

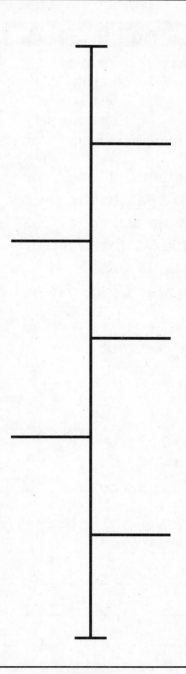

Choosing the Right Words

📖 Use Handbook page 153.

■ **Read the paragraph.**

■ **Rewrite the paragraph. Replace the underlined words with colorful verbs or specific nouns. Add describing words. You might want to use the words in the charts.**

Colorful Verbs	Specific Nouns	Describing Words
grabbed	racket and visor	new
raced	Coach Kraft	near his house
smacked	an hour	bright yellow
ran	tennis match	across the net

Nikolai <u>got</u> his <u>equipment</u>. It was time for his tennis lesson. He <u>went</u> to the park. <u>His teacher</u> was already on the court. He hit the ball to Nikolai. Nikolai <u>hit</u> the ball back. They played for <u>a while</u>, then Nikolai walked home. He was tired, but he really enjoyed the <u>game</u>.

_____

_____

_____

_____

_____

_____

_____

_____

_____

Combining Short Sentences

📖 Use Handbook pages 154–155.

■ **Read the paragraph.**

■ **Rewrite the paragraph. Combine the short sentences.**

     Paula likes to walk. She walks everywhere. She walks her dog every day. Sometimes she takes him to the park. Sometimes she walks him around her neighborhood. Paula walks to the pool. She goes there in the summer. In the winter, she walks to the frozen lake. She goes there to ice skate. On her autumn walks, Paula loves to look at the colorful trees. She loves to breathe in the cold, fresh air. In the spring, Paula walks. She takes long walks. She can see all the new flowers blooming.

Paula likes to walk everywhere. _____

_____

_____

_____

_____

_____

_____

Making Sentences Interesting

Use Handbook pages 154–155.

- ■ **Read the paragraph.**
- ■ **Rewrite the paragraph. Break up sentences that use *and* too many times. Begin some of the sentences in different ways.**

Malcolm loves to swim, and he swims on a swim team and he practices every day of the week for an hour. Malcolm swims four laps of the crawl on Saturdays while Coach Lee times him. Coach writes the time down in a book so they can keep track of it and Malcolm's time gets faster every week. Coach Lee is very proud of how hard Malcolm works. Malcolm is pleased with the results, too, and he got his first ribbon during a swim meet last week, and it was a red one for second place.

Malcolm loves to swim.

_____

_____

_____

_____

_____

_____

_____

_____

_____

Adding Details

📖 Use Handbook page 155.

- Talk about the picture with a partner. Make up a story about it.

- Write the story. Use lots of details to make your story interesting to read.

_____

_____

_____

_____

_____

_____

_____

_____

_____

Showing What You Mean

📖 Use Handbook page 156.

■ **Read each sentence.**

■ **Find the sentence in the box that *shows*
exactly what the writer means. Write it
in the blank.**

> The audience claps loudly after each performance.
> Andrea spends at least two hours every day to get ready for a concert.
> At Andrea's house, you'll always hear someone singing or playing an instrument.
> "I can listen for hours to works by classical musicians like Bach, Chopin, and Beethoven."
> "There is nothing I would rather do than play the piano."

1. Andrea's family loves music.

At Andrea's house, you'll always hear someone singing or playing an instrument.

2. Andrea's favorite music is classical music.

_____

_____

3. Andrea likes to play the piano.

_____

_____

4. She practices a lot.

_____

_____

5. People like when she performs.

_____

_____

Kinds of Sentences

📖 Use Handbook page 160.

- Read each sentence.
- Write an ending from the box to finish each kind of sentence.

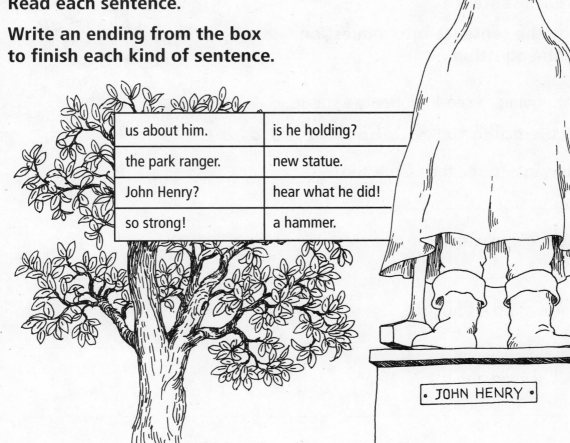

us about him.	is he holding?
the park ranger.	new statue.
John Henry?	hear what he did!
so strong!	a hammer.

1. statement   Here is a *new statue.* _____

2. question   Who is _____

3. command   Ask _____

4. exclamation   The man looks _____

5. question   What _____

6. statement   It looks like _____

7. command   Please tell _____

8. exclamation   I can't wait to _____

Kinds of Sentences

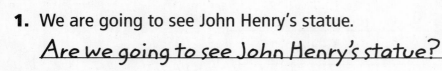

📖 Use Handbook pages 160–161.

- ■ **Read each sentence.**
- ■ **Change the sentence into a question. Write the question.**

1. We are going to see John Henry's statue.

Are we going to see John Henry's statue?

2. Mark wants to see the statue, too.

_____

3. Adela is going with him.

_____

4. The new statue is huge.

_____

5. Mark has read about John Henry.

_____

6. Adela wants to read about John Henry and Pecos Bill.

_____

7. She would enjoy reading the tall tales.

_____

8. Adela could read about the characters in Mark's book.

_____

9. The park will get a statue of Pecos Bill, too.

_____

10. Adela and Mark should come back to see the Pecos Bill statue.

_____

Kinds of Sentences

📖 Use Handbook page 161.

- **Read each statement.**
- **Add a question to the end.**
  Write the question.
- **Can your partner answer each question?**

1. You do know about John Henry.

> *You do know about John Henry,*
> *don't you?*

2. John Henry is a folk hero.

_____

_____

3. He worked on the railroads in West Virginia.

_____

_____

4. John Henry was a powerful man.

_____

5. He could pound steel into rock.

_____

6. He raced a steam drill.

_____

7. The steam drill couldn't beat him.

_____

8. John Henry showed that a man could dig faster than a machine.

_____

_____

Kinds of Sentences

📖 Use Handbook page 162.

■ Look at the picture.

■ Write questions about the picture.

■ Read your questions to a partner. Can your partner answer them?

1. Who *is working on the railroad?* _____

2. Where _____

3. Why _____

4. How many _____

5. When _____

6. How _____

7. Which _____

8. What _____

Kinds of Sentences

📖 Use Handbook page 163.

■ **Work with a partner. Read the story about Paul Bunyan on Handbook page 146.**

■ **Read each question. Write the answer. Use negative words.**

Negative Words	
nowhere	nobody
never	no
no one	none
not	nothing

1. Before Paul built the bunkhouses, did his men have somewhere to sleep? *Before Paul built the bunkhouses, his men had nowhere to sleep.*

2. Were the new bunkhouses small? _____

_____

3. Did anybody walk up to bed? _____

_____

4. Did anyone walk down to breakfast? _____

_____

5. Could any of the cooks flip flapjacks fast enough? _____

_____

6. Did the men ever run out of syrup for their flapjacks? _____

_____

7. Was anything left of the hills when the men leveled the Great Plains? _____

_____

8. Were there any trees left after the men shaved the slopes of the Rocky Mountains? _____

_____

Subject and Predicate

📖 Use Handbook pages 164–165.

■ **Work with a partner.**

■ **Look at the picture. Talk about the tall tale characters.**

■ **Write a subject or a predicate to finish each sentence.**

1. _____Danny and Ellen_____ love to read tall tales.

2. _____ is their favorite tall tale character.

3. Paul _____ .

4. He _____ .

5. Paul's best friend _____ .

6. _____ is a big, blue ox.

7. _____ helped Paul with his work.

8. Babe _____ .

9. _____ made paths through the mountains.

10. Babe and Paul _____ .

Compound Sentences

📖 Use Handbook page 166.

- Read the story.
- Write *and, but,* or *or* to join the two parts of each compound sentence. Use the correct punctuation.

When Pecos Bill was a baby, he was traveling

West with his family, __but__ he fell out of the
            1

wagon. Pecos fell into a river_____ a coyote
                              2

saved him. "I could give him back to the humans_____ I could
                                                    3

raise him as my own," she thought. The coyote took the baby

to her den_____ Pecos Bill learned how to live like a coyote.
          4

One day, Cowboy Hank was out riding on the range_____ his
                                                      5

horse almost stepped on Pecos Bill. Pecos was asleep_____ Hank woke
                                                      6

him up. Hank told Pecos that he was a human_____ Pecos believed he
                                              7

was a coyote. Hank said "I can show you how to be a cowboy_____ you
                                                            8

can stay with the coyotes."

Pecos Bill decided to be a cowboy_____ Hank helped him start
                                  9

a ranch. Soon Pecos had gathered every steer in Texas_____ people
                                                      10

talked about how he was the greatest cowboy in the country.

Singular and Plural Nouns

📖 Use Handbook pages 168–169.

bay	box	coach	butterfly	Sunday	roof

story					cave
man					beach
child					woman
leaf					city
island					person
BEGIN					

**How to Play
The Noun Game**

1. Play with a partner.
2. Use an eraser or small object as your game piece. Use a coin to show how many spaces to move.

   🪙 Heads = 1 space

   🪙 Tails = 2 spaces

3. Read the singular noun.
4. Say the plural noun. Write it on a sheet of paper.
5. The first one to reach THE END wins.

THE END	knife	house	cliff

Singular and Plural Nouns

 Use Handbook pages 168–169.

- **Read the sentence.**
- **Write the word in dark print in the blank. Make the word plural if you need to.**

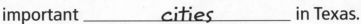

Galveston ★

city   **1.** Galveston is one of the most

important _____ *cities* _____ in Texas.

rice   **2.** From this port, _____ and
other products are shipped to other places.

sugar   **3.** Bananas, _____, and automobiles
are shipped in.

tea   **4.** Galveston produces frozen seafood and
_____ .

visitor   **5.** This city also gets a lot of _____ .

beach   **6.** They like to visit the many _____
along the coast.

temperature   **7.** In the summer, the _____ is around 90°.

water   **8.** That's perfect weather for swimming in the
_____ .

football   **9.** People also like to play _____ in the
city parks.

child   **10.** In April, _____ can go to a special festival.

kite   **11.** At the festival, they can fly all kinds of _____ .

money   **12.** People can have fun in Galveston without spending
a lot of _____ .

Words That Signal Nouns

📖 **Use Handbook pages 170–171.**

- **Read the paragraphs.**
- **Write the word that goes before the noun.**
  Use *a*, *the*, *some*, or *an*.

Luisa loves ___*the*___ ocean. She read _____ interesting article
                    1   2

about it. There is _____ underwater garden 100 miles off the coast
                    3

of Galveston. It is called _____ Flower Garden National Marine
                            4

Sanctuary. _____ marine sanctuary is a place where the fish
            5

and _____ ocean's plants are protected.
     6

_____ kinds of fish that live in the sanctuary are Caribbean reef fish.
 7

The manta ray is _____ animal that lives there, too. The underwater
                  8

garden is also _____ good home for turtles. All the animals swim
                9

around _____ coral reefs and sand flats.
        10

Luisa wants to become _____ marine researcher.
                       11

She wants to study _____ more places like the
                    12

Flower Garden Marine Sanctuary.

Words That Signal Nouns

📖 Use Handbook pages 170–171.

- Read each sentence.
- Write the word *a, the, some,* or *an* to finish the sentence.

1. My family takes _____*a*_____ vacation every year.

2. I think Stewart Beach on Galveston Island is _____ great place to go.

3. We go there in _____ summer.

4. We never forget to take _____ sunscreen.

5. Mom always brings _____ snacks, too.

6. It only takes _____ hour to get there.

7. At the beach, my brother and I always build _____ sandcastles.

8. Sometimes we toss _____ ball back and forth.

9. Then we swim in _____ ocean.

10. My mom sits under _____ umbrella.

11. She enjoys reading _____ good book.

12. Everyone always has _____ good time.

Words That Signal Nouns

📖 Use Handbook page 171.

- Read each sentence.
- Choose the correct word below the line.
- Write the word in the blank.

1. "Galveston has great stores," said Mom. "Let's

   go in ____*that*____ store across the street."

this/that

2. "_____ store is great," I told the

Those/This

   clerk. "Do you have tennis shoes?"

3. "Yes, we do. _____ shoes over by the door are

This/Those

   our latest styles."

4. "If you like shoes with high tops, _____ pair next
   to them is on sale."
that/these

5. "What about _____ pair?" asked Mom.

these/this

6. "_____ shoes fit perfectly," I said.

This/These

7. "Can I get some socks from _____ rack in the back?"

that/those

8. "Sure," said Mom. "_____ socks look just right
   for tennis, too."
Those/This

Possessive Nouns

📖 Use Handbook page 172.

- Read each sentence.
- Add an apostrophe (') and an *s* to the word in dark print to show if there is one owner or more than one owner.
- Write the word in the blank.

TEXAS

Galveston ★

Galveston 1. When you go to _____*Galveston's*_____ shops you can find lots of souvenirs.

friend 2. My three _____ favorite souvenirs are T-shirts.

shirt 3. There are different designs on the _____ fronts.

museum 4. Many shirts have a _____ name on them.

boy 5. Both _____ shirts say "Flight Museum."

girl 6. The _____ shirt says "Galveston Spring Fest."

father 7. My _____ caps are from Galveston, too.

cap 8. The _____ fronts say "Joe's Cafe."

restaurant 9. Dad really likes that _____ food!

mom 10. My _____ favorite souvenirs are hats.

shop 11. We look in all the _____ windows until we find a hat with a ribbon on it.

hat 12. Her _____ ribbon is a beautiful ocean green.

Possessive Nouns

📖 Use Handbook page 172.

- Read each sentence.
- Choose the correct word from below the line.
- Write the word in the blank.

1. On Saturday _____*Michael's*_____ uncle asked Michael and Paul
   Michael's/Michaels'

   what they wanted to see.

2. The boys looked in the _____ brochure.
   hotel's/hotels'

3. The _____ choice was the Tall Ship Elissa.
   boy's/boys'

4. So they went to see the ship at _____ dock.
   Galveston's/Galvestons'

5. Uncle Pete said, "Imagine traveling over an _____
   ocean's/oceans'
   waves without a motor."

6. "It took several sailors to raise that _____ sails."
   ship's/ships'

7. "The _____ jobs must have been hard."
   sailor's/sailors'

8. "Most of the _____ decks were made of hard wood."
   ship's/ships'

9. "The _____ surface must have been uncomfortable to sleep on!"
   deck's/decks'

10. The boys took lots of pictures of the ship with Uncle _____
    camera.   Pete's/Petes'

Using Nouns in Writing

📖 Use Handbook page 173.

■ **Read the paragraph. Look at the underlined words.**

■ **Rewrite the paragraph. Replace the underlined words with specific nouns.**

    In <u>the neighborhood</u> everyone likes to eat out. We go to the <u>restaurant</u>. There you can get good food for lunch or dinner. For lunch, I like to eat a <u>sandwich</u>. I also order a large <u>drink</u>. If we go there for dinner, I usually get <u>pasta</u>. Sometimes I have a <u>vegetable</u>, too. For dessert, you can choose from <u>all the things</u> that are on the menu. I always save room for <u>dessert</u> because it's so good!

_____

_____

_____

_____

_____

_____

_____

_____

_____

_____

_____

_____

Using Different Kinds of Pronouns

📖 Use Handbook pages 174–175.

- ■ **Read the sentences.**
- ■ **Choose the pronoun that goes in each blank. Fill in the circle for the answer.**
- ■ **Write the pronoun on the line.**

Tom

Lisa

Joey

Coach Brown

1. Today is Saturday. _____ is the day we play soccer.   _____*It*_____
  ○ You   ● It   ○ I

2. Mr. Brown blows the whistle. _____ is our soccer coach.   _____
  ○ She   ○ He   ○ It

3. Joey is the goalie. _____ gets into position.   _____
  ○ He   ○ You   ○ I

4. The Rangers run out to the field. _____ are ready for the kick.   _____
  ○ It   ○ They   ○ You

5. "Tom, are _____ ready to receive the ball?" asks Lisa.   _____
  ○ you   ○ I   ○ it

6. "Yes, _____ am!" says Tom.   _____
  ○ I   ○ you   ○ he

7. Lisa runs. _____ kicks the ball to Tom.   _____
  ○ I   ○ They   ○ She

8. "Hooray!" _____ all cheer when Tom kicks the ball into the net.   _____
  ○ He   ○ It   ○ We

Using Different Kinds of Pronouns

📖 Use Handbook page 176.

- **Read the paragraphs. Look at the underlined words.**

- **Rewrite the paragraphs. Use pronouns to take the place of the underlined words.**

Tom

Lisa

Coach Brown

    <u>Last Saturday</u> was the third game of the season. When <u>Tom and Lisa</u> got to the field it started to sprinkle. Coach told <u>Tom and Lisa</u> to try to play anyway. "A little rain shouldn't bother <u>all the Bobcats</u>," Coach told Lisa.
    So <u>Lisa</u> ran out to the field. The rain was falling harder. Tom tried to kick the ball to <u>Lisa</u>, but slipped on the wet grass. The player next to <u>Tom</u> slipped, too. Soon everyone was laughing. The game was cancelled, but <u>the players on both teams</u> all had a great time!

It was the third game of the season. _____

_____

_____

_____

_____

_____

_____

_____

_____

Using Different Kinds of Pronouns

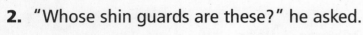 Use Handbook page 177.

- **Read each sentence.**
- **Choose the correct word below the line.**
- **Write the word in the blank.**

1. Coach was cleaning out _____*our*_____ bag of soccer equipment.
   our/ours

2. "Whose shin guards are these?" he asked.

   "Oh, those are _____," said Tom.
   my/mine

    Tom

    Juan

3. "What about this cap? Is it _____, Juan?"
   your/yours

    Lisa

4. "No," said Juan. "I think it's Lisa's. _____ cap is yellow."
   Her/Hers

5. "Jasmine, is this your shoe?"

   "No, it must be Juan's. He lost _____," she said.
   his/hers

    Jasmine

6. "Does this goalie mask belong to the Eagles? I think it's _____,"
   said Tom.
   their/theirs

7. "Finally, here's _____ whistle!" said Coach.
   my/mine

    Coach Brown

8. "Did the dog lose _____ cap?"
   its/it's

9. "Well, _____ not lost anymore."
   its/it's

    Nuff

10. "_____ here, too."
    Its/It's

Using Different Kinds of Pronouns

Use Handbook page 178.

- **Read what Jasmine and her mother are saying.**

- **Use words from the box to finish their sentences. Write the words in the blanks.**

everyone	something	everybody	somebody
anything	someone	everything	anyone

"How was the party after the game?" asked Mom.

" ___Everything___ was great," said Jasmine.
　　　　　　　1

"Was _____ there?"
　　　　　　　2

"_____ on the team came," answered Jasmine.
　　　3

"We were so happy that we won _____."
　　　　　　　　　　　　　　　4

"Did you have _____ to eat?"
　　　　　　　　　　5

"Yes, we did. I don't know who made the oatmeal cookies,

but _____ is a good cook. They were delicious!"
　　　　6

"Did _____ bring a camera?"
　　　　7

"_____ did, but I'm not sure who. I can't wait
　　　8

to see the pictures!"

Using Pronouns in Writing

📖 Use Handbook page 179.

■ **Read the letter. Look at the underlined nouns.**

■ **Rewrite the paragraphs in the letter. Replace each underlined noun with a pronoun from the box.**

Pronouns			
he	she	it	they
his	him	their	them

575 Hannon St.
Dallas, TX 75201
September 12, 2002

Dear Joseph,

How's soccer? I got a letter from Tom. Tom said that the Bobcats are playing the Eagles next week. The Eagles will be hard to beat.

I remember when we played against the Eagles. The Eagles' goalie is really good. Mike is Mike's name. It's hard to get a ball past Mike. There's also a player named Melissa. Melissa is a fast runner!

Good luck in your game. I hope you win the game!

Your pal,
Ramon

_____

_____

_____

_____

_____

_____

_____

Using Adjectives to Describe

📖 Use Handbook page 180.

- ■ **Look at the picture.**
- ■ **Read each sentence.**
- ■ **Write a word from the chart to finish the sentence.**

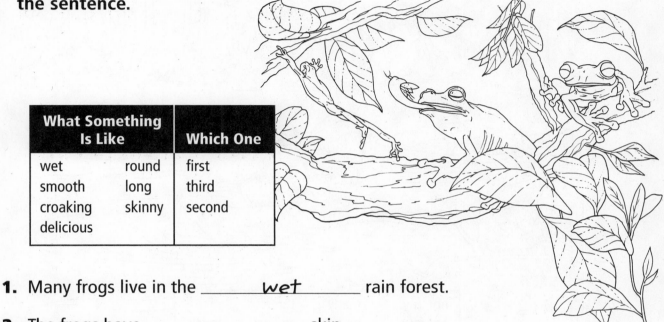

What Something Is Like		Which One
wet	round	first
smooth	long	third
croaking	skinny	second
delicious		

1. Many frogs live in the _____ *wet* _____ rain forest.

2. The frogs have _____ skin.

3. Their eyes are big and _____.

4. The _____ frog is jumping to a different branch.

5. The _____ frog is catching a bug.

6. The frog uses its _____ tongue to catch it.

7. A bug tastes _____ to a frog.

8. The _____ frog is sleeping.

9. It hangs onto the branch with its _____ toes.

10. I wonder if the frog makes a _____ sound when it sleeps!

Using Adjectives to Describe

📖 Use Handbook page 181.

■ **Look at the picture.**

■ **Read each sentence.**

■ **Write a word from the box to finish the sentence.**

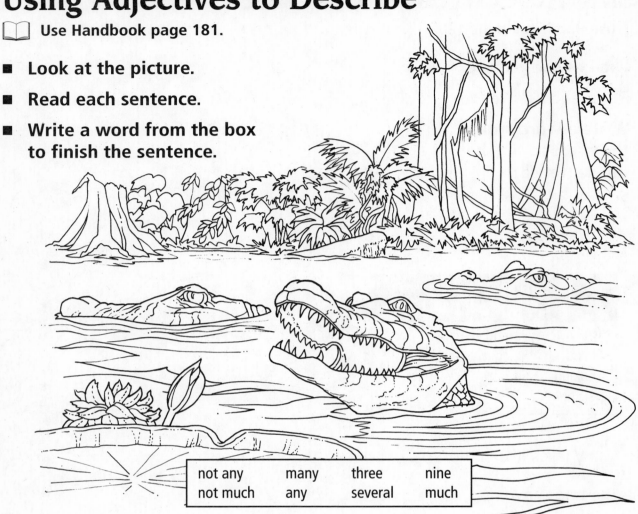

| not any | many | three | nine |
| not much | any | several | much |

1. These _____*three*_____ big caimans look like alligators.

2. They have _____ teeth!

3. It's funny how they float with _____ of their body showing.

4. It is amazing that they do not swallow _____ water.

5. Can you believe that a baby caiman is just _____ inches long?

6. Caimans grow up to be _____ bigger!

7. Caimans eat _____ kinds of animals.

8. No wonder there are _____ monkeys nearby!

Using Adjectives to Compare

📖 Use Handbook pages 182–183.

- **Look at the pictures.**
- **Read each sentence. Write the correct word in the blank.**

jaguar   puma   ocelot

1. The jaguar is the _____*largest*_____ wild cat in the Americas.
   larger/largest

2. It is also the _____ powerful of the cats.
   more/most

3. With its golden or brownish yellow spots, the jaguar is _____ colorful than the puma.
   more/most

4. The ocelot has _____ spots, too.
   more/some

5. The ocelot and the puma are _____ climbers than the jaguar.
   better/best

6. The ocelot and the jaguar are _____ swimmers.
   good/best

7. An adult jaguar usually weighs _____ than a puma.
   more/most

8. The puma is _____ than a jaguar.
   thinner/thinnest

9. The ocelot weighs the _____ amount of all.
   less/least

10. It's the _____ wild cat.
    smaller/smallest

Name _____ Date _____

Using Adjectives in Writing

📖 Use Handbook page 185.

- Talk about the picture with a partner.

- Write sentences to tell about the
  plants and animals. Use lots of adjectives.

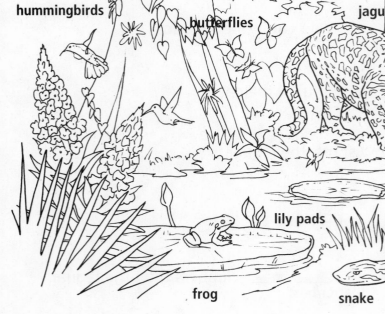

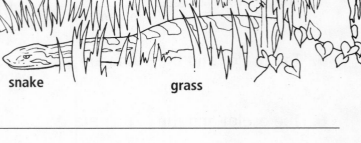

_____

_____

_____

_____

_____

_____

_____

_____

_____

Action Verbs

📖 **Use Handbook page 186.**

- **Read each sentence.**
- **Write the correct verb from the box in the blank.**

1. I _____ like _____ the autumn.

2. At that time of year, the temperature _____ to 45 degrees.

3. The leaves _____ different colors.

4. They _____ off the trees.

5. The wind _____ the leaves all around.

6. I _____ outside in the cool, crisp air.

like
turn
drops
fall
blows
play

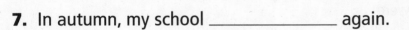

7. In autumn, my school _____ again.

8. Dad _____ me up early.

9. My sister and I _____ breakfast.

10. Then we _____ on the bus.

11. At school I _____ friends that I haven't seen all summer.

12. We all _____ to new classrooms with new teachers.

wakes
ride
go
see
eat
starts

Linking Verbs

📖 Use Handbook page 186.

- ■ **Read each sentence.**
- ■ **Choose the correct verb below the line. Write the verb in the blank.**

1. I _____*am*_____ a cloud watcher.

am/is

2. Look! There _____ some fluffy, white clouds.

is/are

3. One cloud _____ in the shape of a dragon!

is/are

4. Yesterday there _____ gray rain clouds in the sky.

was/were

5. After it rained, there _____ a beautiful rainbow.

was/were

6. Heavy, dark clouds _____ in the sky last week.

was/were

7. I knew then that snow _____ on its way.

was/were

8. Now you know why clouds _____ interesting to watch.

is/are

9. They _____ clues that tell what the weather will be like.

is/are

10. I _____ curious about what the clouds will tell me

am/is

    about the weather tomorrow.

Helping Verbs

📖 Use Handbook page 187.

■ **Read each sentence.**

■ **Write the correct verb from the box in the blank.**

■ **Circle the helping verb in each answer.**

1. Early this morning, the sun _____(was) shining_____.

2. By 11 a.m., however, the weather _____.

3. Blankets of gray clouds _____ the sun.

4. The temperature _____.

5. I thought it _____.

6. At 2 p.m., snowflakes _____ to fall.

did start
had changed
was shining
were blocking
might snow
had dropped

7. We _____ it snow from the window.

8. The snow _____ the ground.

9. "We _____ outside to play," I said to my sister.

10. "We _____ a snow castle!"

11. My sister _____ her coat already.

12. She _____ out the door.

can build
was running
were watching
should go
had grabbed
was covering

Present-Tense Verbs

📖 Use Handbook pages 188–189.

- Read each sentence.
- Write the correct form of the word in dark print in the blank.

enjoy   1. In our neighborhood, we ____enjoy____ all kinds of weather.

love   2. Eric _____ the rain.

watch   3. He _____ it pour down from his window.

try   4. Anna _____ to catch the rain in a bucket so she can measure it.

like   5. I _____ the winter months.

freeze   6. The lake _____ then.

skate   7. My friend and I _____ on the frozen lake.

ride   8. In the spring, all the kids _____ their bikes.

ask   9. Sometimes my dad _____ "Can I go with you?"

swim   10. During hot weather, Juan _____ every day.

sell   11. Sue and Joli are smart! They _____ us lemonade on those hot days.

taste   12. The cool lemonade _____ great!

Present-Tense Verbs

📖 Use Handbook pages 188–189.

■ **Look at each picture. Read the sentences.**

■ **Add _–ing_ to the verb to tell what the people are doing. Write the verb in the blank.**

1. swim Manuel is ___swimming___ in the pool.

2. wear He is _____ goggles.

5. walk Mia and Grandmother are _____ in the rain.

6. hold They are _____ umbrellas.

3. run Vi is _____ across a field.

4. fly She is _____ a kite.

7. come Jamal is _____ down the hill.

8. sled He is _____ on the snow.

Past-Tense Verbs

📖 Use Handbook page 190.

■ **Read each question.**

■ **Add _-ed_ to the underlined verb to make it tell about the past.**

■ **Use the past-tense verb to finish the answer.**

1. Did you <u>watch</u> the weather report last night?

   Yes, we _watched the weather report last night._____

2. Did the scientists <u>gather</u> information for it?

   Yes, the scientists _____

3. Did they <u>study</u> the weather patterns?

   Yes, they _____

4. Did they <u>use</u> many tools?

   Yes, they _____

5. Did the balloons <u>stay</u> in the air to measure the wind speeds?

   Yes, the balloons _____

   _____

6. Did the weather satellites <u>snap</u> pictures of the clouds?

   Yes, the weather satellites _____

   _____

7. Did the tools <u>measure</u> wind, air, and temperature?

   Yes, the tools _____

8. Did the reporter <u>predict</u> the weather?

   Yes, the reporter _____

Past-Tense Verbs

📖 Use Handbook page 191.

- ■ **Read the paragraph. Look at the underlined words.**

- ■ **Rewrite the paragraph to make it tell about an action that happened in the past.**

How <u>do</u> some people predict the weather? Everyday things and animals <u>give</u> them clues. Some people <u>say</u> to look at the color of the sky. A dark, cloudy sky <u>brings</u> rain or snow. A clear, blue sky <u>is</u> a sign of fair weather ahead. Other people <u>find</u> a clue from the groundhog. If the groundhog <u>sees</u> its shadow, there'd be six more weeks of winter. Spring <u>begins</u> if the groundhog could not see its shadow. On the seacoast, people <u>keep</u> seaweed hanging near their houses. The seaweed <u>gets</u> dry in clear weather. A clump of wool <u>holds</u> moisture in rainy weather. During stormy weather some animals <u>hide</u> in caves. Other animals <u>go</u> underground. There <u>are</u> clues everywhere!

How did some people predict the weather? _____

_____

_____

_____

_____

_____

_____

_____

_____

_____

_____

Past-Tense Verbs

📖 Use Handbook page 191.

- Read each sentence.
- Change the verb below the blank to make it tell about the past.
- Write the past-tense verb in the blank.

1. It _____was_____ so hot in New Mexico!
   be

2. The temperature _____ up to 95 degrees.
   get

3. We _____ we would burn up in the sun.
   think

4. We _____ cool and safe though.
   keep

5. Mom _____ lots of sunscreen.
   bring

6. We _____ special hats to wear.
   find

7. The hats _____ perfect!
   be

8. The brims _____ our faces from the sun.
   hide

9. We _____ lots of water.
   drink

10. I _____ plenty of ice in mine!
    keep

11. We _____ swimming, too.
    go

12. There _____ a nice, cool pool at our hotel.
    be

Future-Tense Verbs

📖 Use Handbook page 192.

- **What is the boy going to do in the future?**

- **Choose words from the box to finish each sentence.**

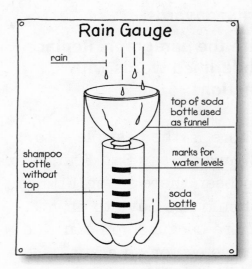

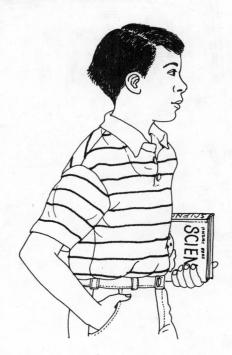

1. Tomorrow, Tran _____*will make*_____ a rain gauge.

2. He _____ an old plastic bottle.

3. The marks on the bottle _____ different water levels.

4. "I _____ the gauge outside," said Tran.

5. "The rain _____ into the gauge."

6. "I _____ at the water level every morning."

7. "I _____ the number of inches to see how much rain falls."

8. "The gauge _____, though, if it doesn't rain!"

will make
am going to put
will fall
will look
is going to use
are going to show
will write
won't work

Contractions with Verbs

📖 Use Handbook page 193.

- **Read the paragraph. Look at the underlined words.**

- **Rewrite the paragraph. Replace the underlined words with contractions.**

Where is the best place to visit? I would say San Francisco. I have been there several times. You should not have to drive anywhere because you can ride on a cable car or on a bus. You will love walking down the steep, crooked streets! Do not miss the Golden Gate Bridge! You cannot leave without seeing it. The weather is not too cold, but take a jacket. It is cool and sometimes foggy at night. You will not be disappointed when you go to San Francisco!

Where's the best place to visit? _____

_____

_____

_____

_____

_____

_____

_____

_____

Using Verbs in Writing

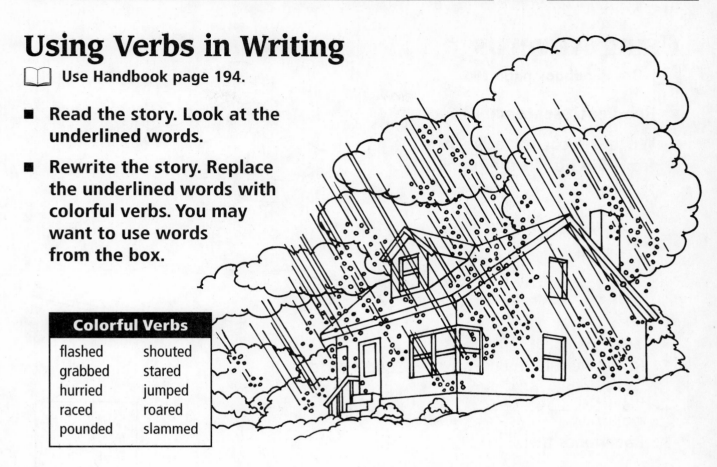

 Use Handbook page 194.

- **Read the story. Look at the underlined words.**

- **Rewrite the story. Replace the underlined words with colorful verbs. You may want to use words from the box.**

Colorful Verbs

flashed	shouted
grabbed	stared
hurried	jumped
raced	roared
pounded	slammed

One morning, I <u>got</u> out of bed. "What's that noise?" I <u>said</u>. I <u>got</u> my slippers. Then I <u>went</u> to the window. I <u>looked</u> outside. Lightning <u>was</u> in the sky. Then the thunder <u>came</u>. After that, balls of hail <u>were</u> against the house. I <u>put</u> the window down just in time! I <u>moved</u> back into my warm, cozy bed.

One morning, I jumped out of bed. _____

_____

_____

_____

_____

_____

_____

Using Adverbs

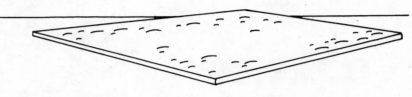
Use Handbook page 195.

■ **Read each sentence.**

■ **Write the correct adverb from the box in the blank.**

1. Roger went to the new gym _____*yesterday*_____ .

2. It's nice _____ the gym.

3. Roger goes there _____ to practice.

4. He jumped _____ to reach the rings.

5. He swung _____ back and forth on the rings.

6. Roger's arms are _____ strong.

| slowly |
| inside |
| really |
| yesterday |
| high |
| often |

---

7. Then Roger swung back and forth _____.

8. He brought his legs _____ and flipped all the way around!

9. He let go and flew _____ the rings.

10. He landed _____ on the soft mat.

11. Roger is a _____ good gymnast.

12. He _____ performs well.

| very |
| always |
| perfectly |
| up |
| off |
| more quickly |

Using Adverbs to Compare

 Use Handbook page 196.

■ **Read each sentence.**

■ **Choose the correct word below the line.
Write the word in the blank.**

1. This floor show is _____*longer*_____
   than last year's.   longer/longest

2. Look! Ciara is tumbling

   _____ than Lu.
   faster/fastest

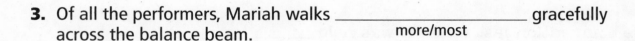

3. Of all the performers, Mariah walks _____ gracefully
   across the balance beam.   more/most

4. Of all the gymnasts I know, Beto loses his balance on the high beam

   the _____ frequently.
   less/least

5. He is also _____ careful than Jason on the rings.
   more/most

6. Lu finishes the floor exercise _____ of all the competitors.
   faster/fastest

7. The coaches look _____ worried today than they
   did yesterday.   less/least

8. The judges are the _____ I have ever met.
   friendlier/friendliest

9. The audience is clapping _____ loudly than they
   ever have before.   more/most

10. I think everyone performed very _____, don't you?
    good/well

Using Adverbs in Writing

📖 **Use Handbook page 197.**

always	really
inside	highest
more carefully	often
well	perfectly

■ **Read the letter.**

■ **Write an adverb from the box for each blank.**

683 Willow Rd.
Los Angeles, CA 90015
March 6, 2001

Dear Bill,

    Our gymnastic team did very _____ *well* _____ in
                1

the competition last week. It was held _____
                               2

the new gym on Oak Street.

    It was _____ exciting to see Ciara
                 3

perform. She walked _____ across the beam
                       4

than anyone else. Beto jumped the _____ of
                             5

all the gymnasts during the floor exercise. Jason tumbled

_____, too.
     6

    I know you don't travel _____, but
                          7

maybe you'll come to see us. I _____ want
                         8

to show off my team! I hope to see you soon.

               Your friend,

               Coach Raphael

Ways to Use Prepositions

📖 Use Handbook page 198.

- Look at the picture.
- Read each sentence.
- Write a word from the box to tell where things are.

1. The children's kites are _____*in*_____ the sky.

2. There's a picture of a dragon _____ the boy's kite.

3. The girl's kite is _____ the boy's kite and a tree.

4. Her kite is right _____ the tree.

5. Oh no! It's going to crash _____ the tree!

6. There's a kite already _____ the tree!

7. That kite's tail is wrapped _____ a branch.

8. Will someone get the kite's tail _____ the branch?

| inside |
| on |
| next to |
| between |
| off |
| in |
| into |
| around |

Ways to Use Prepositions

📖 Use Handbook page 198.

- Read each sentence.
- Choose the preposition that goes in the sentence. Fill in the circle for the answer.
- Write the preposition on the line.

1. There is going to be a Kite Festival _____ April 24.   _____ on _____
   ● on   ○ in   ○ from

2. It's going to be held _____ 10 a.m. to 7 p.m.   _____
   ○ from   ○ until   ○ for

3. Children should sign up for the kite-flying contest   _____
   _____ noon.
   ○ in   ○ before   ○ on

4. There will be lots of games to play _____ the day, too.   _____
   ○ from   ○ to   ○ during

5. The kite-flying contest will be held _____ 2 p.m.   _____
   ○ in   ○ after   ○ from

6. Later _____ the afternoon there will be a kite-making   _____
   workshop.
   ○ in   ○ on   ○ without

7. Awards will be given out from 3:30 p.m. _____ 4:30 p.m.   _____
   ○ during   ○ to   ○ with

8. When the awards are over, there'll be a picnic that will   _____
   last _____ dark.
   ○ until   ○ from   ○ on

Using Prepositions in Writing

📖 Use Handbook page 199.

- **Read the story.**

- **Add details to the story.
  Use prepositional phrases
  from the boxes.**

_____In August_____, Dad and I went to
      1

Chicago. It was my first trip _____.
                                        2

We got to the airport _____ in the
                              3

morning. We went _____ and
                          4

showed our tickets. Then we walked

_____ to our gate.
      5

| on an airplane |
| to the counter |
| at 10 o'clock |
| In August |
| down a hallway |

_____

When we got on the airplane, we found two seats

_____. We pushed our small
      6

suitcases _____ and sat down.
                7

We buckled our seat belts _____.
                                  8

Soon the airplane lifted _____.
                                9

We flew for an hour and landed in Chicago

_____.
      10

| under the seats |
| off the ground |
| around our laps |
| next to each other |
| before noon |

Name _____ **Date** _____

Using Conjunctions in Writing

📖 Use Handbook page 201.

■ **Read the paragraph.**

■ **Rewrite the paragraph. Use a comma and the conjunction**
and, but, or *or* **to join the short sentences.**

I love sports. Basketball is my favorite.
I like the Coyotes. I like the Falcons better.
Last Saturday I went to a Falcons–Coyotes
game. I sat with the Falcons' fans.

It was the last two minutes of the
game. The score was tied. The Falcons made
a basket. I cheered. Then the Coyotes made
a basket. The Falcons tried for another
basket. The Coyotes blocked them. The
Falcons could give up. They could try again.
The Falcons really wanted to win so they took
another shot. The Coyotes tried to block it.
The ball dropped into the basket. The Falcons
won in the last five seconds of the game!

I love sports, but basketball is my favorite.

_____

_____

_____

_____

_____

_____

_____

_____

_____

_____

Capital Letters

📖 Use Handbook pages 202–203.

■ **Read the announcement.**

■ **Rewrite the announcement. Use capital letters correctly.**

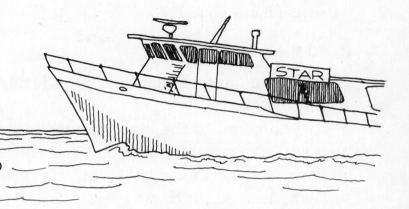

---

1. Join captain Michael s. riley for whale-watching on the Star Cruiser.

2. his crew will answer Any questions about whales.

3. ms. lisa Ramírez

4. mr. Samuel thal

5. Dr. richard zauk

6. what does one passenger say?

7. "it's a great trip."

8. "i can't wait to go again."

9. "next time, i will take my mom and dad."

10. All aboard! we sail at 9 a.m. sharp.

Join Captain Michael S. Riley for whale-watching on the Star Cruiser.

Capital Letters

📖 **Use Handbook page 204.**

■ **Read the paragraph.**

■ **Rewrite the paragraph. Use capital letters correctly.**

If you come to the state of virginia, you'll see a lot of history. Take a boat ride along the chesapeake bay and up the james river. Stop at jamestown, the first permanent English settlement in america. It is part of the colonial national historic park. There you can explore life-size models of three historic ships. Settlers from england sailed here on the susan constant, the godspeed, and the discovery. Take a short drive on the colonial parkway. If you stop at a place called colonial williamsburg, you'll find out how the colonists lived around the time of the American Revolution. So come and visit, and bring your camera!

If you come to the state of Virginia, you'll see a lot of history.

Capital Letters

📖 Use Handbook page 205.

- **Look at the chart.**

- **Read each address on the left. Rewrite the address on the right. Use abbreviations.**

Elena Garcia
218 Sedgewick Pl.
Medford, NJ 08055

Amy Burke
19 Danford St.
Chicago, IL 60625

	Address Without Abbreviations	Address With Abbreviations
1.	Gigi Gallego 302 East San Antonio Drive Seaside, California 93955	Gigi Gallego 302 E. San Antonio Dr. Seaside, CA 93955
2.	Paul Timmins 11479 Rodeo Boulevard San Antonio, Texas 78249	
3.	Joan Matthews 47 South Pelican Street Orlando, Florida 32817	
4.	Frank Miller 98 Washington Square New York, New York 10107	
5.	Andy Ibarra 867 Freedom Lane Boston, Massachusetts 02125	
6.	Brandon Blake 36 West University Avenue Madison, Wisconsin 53706	
7.	Lucas Inouye 44 Kapa Kapa Court Honolulu, Hawaii 96822	
8.	Amanda Rydell 2284 North Covington Place Lincoln, Nebraska 68505	

Capital Letters

📖 Use Handbook page 206.

■ Read the sentences.

■ Rewrite the sentences. Use capital letters correctly.

1. Starting in september, Shawna will be very busy.

   Starting in September,

   Shawna will be very busy.

   _____

2. On labor day, her family is having a big picnic.

   _____

   _____

3. She has a girl scout meeting on the first thursday of the month.

   _____

4. The Milltown science club meets the following Friday.

   _____

5. Shawna's basketball team, the tigers, plays against the eagles a week later.

   _____

6. On sept. 30, she's going with Mom to bill's party supplies and andre's bakery.

   _____

7. They'll shop for her brother's birthday party, which will be at his cub scout meeting on saturday.

   _____

8. Then it'll be october and all Shawna has to do is get ready for halloween!

   _____

Sentence Punctuation

📖 **Use Handbook page 208.**

- **Read each sentence.**
- **Write the correct punctuation mark at the end of the sentence.**

> **HELP WANTED:** Community Center needs help cleaning the grounds. Weekends only. $2.00 per hour. Call 555-5443.

1. I wish I had a way to earn some money___

2. Wow, look at this ad in the newspaper___

3. This job looks perfect for us___

4. What does it say___

5. The Community Center is looking for helpers___

6. What do they want the helpers to do___

7. They want help cleaning up the park___

8. How much are they paying___

9. They will pay the helpers $2.00 an hour___

10. When do they want people to work___

11. They can use help on the weekends___

12. That sounds great___

13. Let's go down there, right now___

14. Do you think any of our friends want to help___

15. Sure. Let's ask Ramon, Sylvia, and Judy___

16. Okay, then, let's go___

The Period and the Comma

📖 Use Handbook page 209.

- ■ **Read the letter.**
- ■ **Use the proofreading marks to add the missing periods and commas.**

Proofreading Marks	
⋀	Add a comma.
⊙	Add a period.

17 North Avenue

New York⋀NY 10033

November 18 2000

Dear Aunt Ruth

Thank you for the wonderful birthday present! Your check for $20.00 was just what I needed to buy some skates. With the $1500 I earned by walking Mr Davi's dog raking leaves and running errands I can buy the skates. They are on sale for $3500.

You'd really like the skates. They are black with red wheels blue shoelaces and silver stripes. My friends Tiffany Max Pablo and B J all have skates. I hope we can skate 1000000 miles!

Thank you again. I can't wait to see you when you visit us again on July 9 2001.

Love

Kelly

The Comma

Use Handbook pages 210–211.

■ **Read what the people are saying.**

■ **Use the proofreading mark to add the missing commas.**

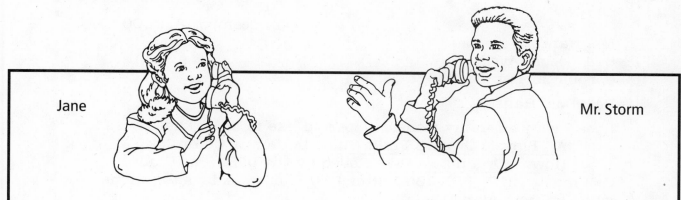

Jane   Mr. Storm

This is the Dog Information Hot Line⋏isn't it?

Yes it is. I'm Mr. Storm.

Mr. Storm my name is Jane. I'm walking a big brown dog named Buster. He's a great dog but he's very hard to handle. My friend Aaron said "Call the Hot Line and they'll help you." You do give people advice don't you?

Yes, I do. Use a six-foot-long strong leash when you walk the dog and hold it with both hands. As my wife says "Keep the dog close so you can handle him better."

Thanks Mr. Storm. I'll ask his owners if they have the right kind of leash or I'll get one myself.

Good. Let me know how you're doing won't you?

Oh you bet I will. Thanks again.

The Colon and the Apostrophe

📖 Use Handbook pages 211–212.

■ **Rewrite the letter. Add the missing colons and apostrophes.**

177 North Avenue
New York, NY 10033
December 3, 2000

Ms. Hansons Books
814 Locust Ave.
Corpus Christi, TX 78374

Dear Ms. Hanson

I read your ad in my fathers paper. Id like to order these books
1. <u>All Bicycle Owners Fix-It Guide</u> by Donna Quinn
2. <u>How to Organize a Bike Rodeo</u> by the U. S. Bike Club

Call me at (212) 555-3399 after 330 p.m. weekdays to tell me
when youre mailing them.

Sincerely,

Aaron Jackson

_____

_____

_____

_____

_____

_____

_____

_____

_____

_____

_____

_____

_____

Underline and Quotation Marks

Use Handbook page 213.

- Read the story.
- Add the missing underlines and quotation marks.

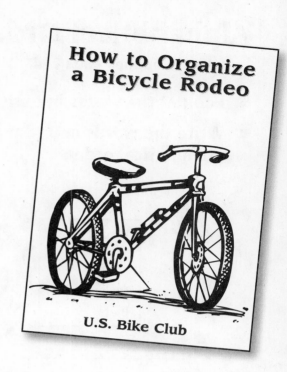

How to Organize a Bicycle Rodeo

U.S. Bike Club

Aaron and his friends read the chapters in Aaron's book, How to Organize a Bike Rodeo. Bobby and Max read "Best Places for a Rodeo." Sam read Advertising the Rodeo. Pablo and Aaron read Games and Prizes. Then they all met to talk about it.

Let's ask Mr. Liu if we can have the rodeo at the school next Saturday, said Aaron. It has a big, safe parking lot.

Okay, said Max. I'll ask The Daily News or Pinewood Gazette to do ads for us.

Maybe the bike shop will give us the prizes. I'll check, said Bobby.

The boys got ready for the rodeo. They made up a song called Ride, Ride, Ride Your Bike. They made up a sign like the one in the book. The sign said, Bicycle Rodeo. Fun for All! They cleaned the school parking lot.

After the rodeo was over, Aaron said, That was a lot of fun.

It was a great idea," said Mr. Liu. I think we should do it every year!"

Alphabetical Order

 Use Handbook page 224.

- Look at the words in each box.
- Write the words in alphabetical order.

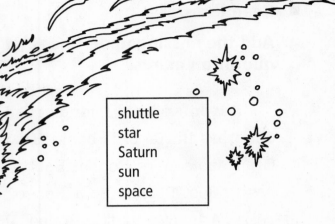

Venus
Mars
Earth
Neptune
Pluto

shuttle
star
Saturn
sun
space

1. *Earth* _____

2. _____

3. _____

4. _____

5. _____

11. _____

12. _____

13. _____

14. _____

15. _____

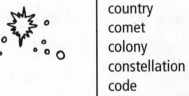

mineral
mud
meteor
matter
moisture

country
comet
colony
constellation
code

6. _____

7. _____

8. _____

9. _____

10. _____

16. _____

17. _____

18. _____

19. _____

20. _____

How to Take Notes

📖 Use Handbook pages 226–227.

- **Read each question.**
- **Write the answer.**

1. Why should you take notes when you read or research a topic?
   to help you remember the facts and details _____

2. What should you do to show that you copied the exact words from something you read?
   _____

3. Look at the notecards on page 227. What is the research question?
   _____

4. What comes after the research question?
   _____

5. Why should you write down the title, author, and page number of a book?
   _____

6. Who wrote the book *Mars*?
   _____

7. Where on the notecards should you write the details and facts you find?
   _____

8. What is one fact from the book *Mars*?
   _____

9. Where can you find the article "Next Stop: Mars"?
   _____

10. Which fact shows exact words copied from a source? Write the fact.
    _____

How to Take Notes

📖 Use Handbook pages 226–227.

- Read the article on Handbook page 225.
- Use the notecards to take notes.

What have scientists learned about life on other planets?
The World Almanac for Kids 1998, page 159

—

—

—

How are scientists searching for life on other planets?

—

—

—

Make an Outline

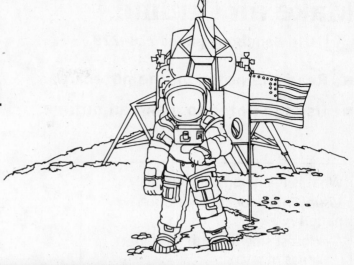

📖 Use Handbook pages 228–229.

- **Read the Main Ideas, Details, and Related Details in the chart.**

- **Finish the outline for a research report about the first moon landing.**

Main Ideas	Details	Related Details
What the astronauts did First humans land on moon	July 20, 1969 American astronauts Took pictures Lunar module called <u>Eagle</u> Left American flag in ground	Neil Armstrong Edwin Aldrin Rocks Soil

A Trip to the Moon

I. _____

   A. *American astronauts* _____

      1. _____

      2. _____

   B. _____

   C. _____

II. _____

   A. *Collected samples* _____

      1. _____

      2. _____

   B. _____

   C. _____

Make an Outline

📖 Use Handbook pages 228–229.

■ **Read the notes on the notecards.**

■ **Use the notes to make an outline.**

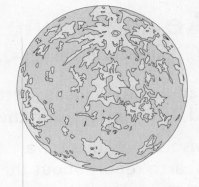

On the Moon

I. *The moon's surface* _____

   A. _____

      1. _____

         _____

      2. _____

         _____

   B. _____

      1. _____

         _____

      2. _____

         _____

II. _____

   A. _____

      _____

   B. _____

      1. _____

         _____

      2. _____

         _____

What is the moon's surface like?
Visual Encyclopedia of Science,
page 176
— closest side to Earth has large
  areas of lava
— farthest side has huge craters
  and mountains

What is the moon's surface like?
World Book Encyclopedia, Vol. 13,
page 784
— near side has flat plains and
  rocky soil
— far side called the highlands,
  it's mountainous

Does the moon have an atmosphere?
Visual Encyclopedia of Science,
page 177
— no atmosphere
— without wind or weather,
  astronauts' footprints last a
  long time

Does the moon have an atmosphere?
World Book Encyclopedia, Vol. 13,
page 788
— little or no atmosphere
— no weather, clouds, rain, or wind
— no air to carry sound, astronauts
  use radios

Card Catalog

Use Handbook pages 234–235.

■ **Read each question.**

■ **Write the answer.**

1. How can you find out if the library has a book you want?

   <u>Look for a card about the book</u>
   <u>in the card catalog.</u>

2. Does the copyright date give the year a book was published or the number of pages in a book?

   _____

3. What number tells you what section of the library a book is in?

   _____

4. How do you know if a book is in the children's section?

   _____

5. What does **KIT** stand for in the call number for Satoshi Kitamura's book?

   _____

6. How are fiction books arranged on the library shelves?

   _____

7. How do you know if a book is in the nonfiction section of the library?

   _____

8. Would you find the book *Are We Moving to Mars?* in the library shelves with other books about the subject "Technology" or "Literature"?

   _____

Card Catalog

📖 **Use Handbook page 236.**

■ **Look at the cards from a card catalog.**

■ **Answer the questions.**

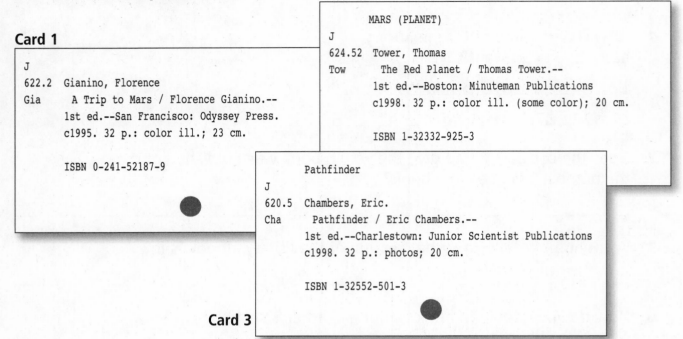

Card 1

```
J
622.2  Gianino, Florence
Gia      A Trip to Mars / Florence Gianino.--
         1st ed.--San Francisco: Odyssey Press.
         c1995. 32 p.: color ill.; 23 cm.

         ISBN 0-241-52187-9
```

Card 2

```
       MARS (PLANET)
J
624.52  Tower, Thomas
Tow       The Red Planet / Thomas Tower.--
          1st ed.--Boston: Minuteman Publications
          c1998. 32 p.: color ill. (some color); 20 cm.

          ISBN 1-32332-925-3
```

Card 3

```
       Pathfinder
J
620.5  Chambers, Eric.
Cha      Pathfinder / Eric Chambers.--
         1st ed.--Charlestown: Junior Scientist Publications
         c1998. 32 p.: photos; 20 cm.

         ISBN 1-32552-501-3
```

1. Is **Card 1** an author card or a title card? *author card* _____

2. Is **Card 2** a subject card or an author card? _____

3. How do you know that the book on **Card 2** is nonfiction? _____

   _____

4. What kind of card is **Card 3**? _____

5. Who wrote the book on **Card 2**? _____

6. What book did Florence Gianino write? _____

7. Would a subject card for PLUTO come before or after the card for MARS? _____

8. Would a card for a book by Mary Borgia come before or after the card

   for the book by Florence Gianino? _____

Parts of a Book: Title Page and Table of Contents

Use Handbook pages 240–241.

Look at Handbook pages 240–241.
Then follow the directions for each part below.

- **Find the Title Page in the front of your Handbook.**
- **Finish the sentences.**

1. The title of the book is _____

2. The publisher is _____ .

_____

- **Look at the Table of Contents on Handbook pages 4–9.**
- **Finish the sentences.**

3. Chapter 1 is mostly about _____ .

4. Chapter 2 begins on _____ .

5. In Chapter 2, the kinds of graphs you can read about are _____
   _____ .

6. Three kinds of writing you can find out about in Chapter 3 are _____
   _____ .

7. Chapter 4 is all about _____ .

8. The chapter that tells about finding information on the Internet
   is _____ .

9. The section that begins on page 220 is called _____ .

10. The Index begins on _____ .

Parts of a Book: Index

📖 Use Handbook page 242.

- **Read about an index on Handbook page 242.**
- **Turn to Handbook pages 328–335.**
- **Answer the questions.**

1. How are subjects listed in an index?

in alphabetical order _____

2. Does the subject "Book review" come before or after

the subject "Biography"? _____

3. What are the related details listed for the subject "Letters"?

_____

_____

4. On which pages can you find information about business letters?

_____

5. Find the pages about business letters. Name the parts of a business letter.

_____

_____

6. Find "World Wide Web" in the index. What other subject does it say to look up?

_____

7. On which pages can you find information about the subject "Internet"?

_____

8. Look up the pages about the "Internet." Which page tells you what
the World Wide Web is? What is the World Wide Web?

_____

_____

Parts of a Book: Glossary

📖 Use Handbook page 243.

■ **Work with a partner.**

■ **Write the words in the box in alphabetical order. Then look up each kind of writing in Chapter 3 of the Handbook.**

■ **Write a definition for each entry to make a glossary.**

Kinds of Writing	
Fairy Tale	Autobiography
Play	Tall Tale
Personal Narrative	Fantasy
Folk Tale	Biography

GLOSSARY

1. Autobiography — the true story of your own life, written by you.

2. _____

3. _____

4. _____

5. _____

6. _____

7. _____

8. _____

Almanac

📖 Use Handbook pages 244–245.

■ **What is an almanac like?
How can you use it?**

■ **Finish the sentences to tell about
an almanac.**

1. An almanac is a _____ *book of facts* _____.
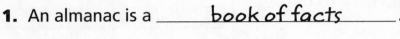

2. It has information about many different
   _____.

3. An almanac has up-to-date information because it is rewritten
   _____.

4. To find out if an almanac has information about a subject, first look up
   key words in the _____.

5. Then turn to _____ for the article in the book.

6. Next, _____ the article to see if it has the
   information you want.

7. Use the _____ and the _____
   in the article to find the main ideas.

8. Look for _____ and _____
   in dark print.

9. Also look for _____ , _____ ,
   and _____ that might have useful information.

10. If the article is useful for your report, _____
    and _____.

Almanac

📖 Use Handbook pages 244–245.

- **Read the questions.**
- **Use the almanac pages in your Handbook to answer the questions.**

1. How can you find the article in the almanac?

look up the key words in the index

2. What is the title of the article? _____

3. Under which heading can you find out how planets move?

_____

4. What key words can you find on the first page of the article?

_____

5. What is an *axis*?

_____

6. What does the diagram on the second page of the article show?

_____

7. Look at the lists. Is Earth or Mars farther from the sun? _____

8. How long does it take for Earth to revolve around the sun?

_____

9. Look at the special features. What is one interesting fact you learned?

_____

_____

10. Would you read these pages carefully if you were researching facts about the Earth? Why or why not?

_____

_____

Atlas: Physical and Political Maps

📖 Use Handbook pages 246–247.

■ **Read the questions.**

■ **Use the maps in your Handbook to answer the questions.**

1. What does a physical map show?

   the rivers, forests, mountains, lowlands, coastlines,
   or oceans of a place

2. What does a map scale show?

   _____

3. What are the names of the landforms shown on the physical map?

   _____

   _____

4. What does a political map show?

   _____

5. What is the first step in finding a place on a political map?

   _____

6. What special code would you use to find the city of Brunswick

   on the map? _____

7. Will the letter in a special code like **H-5** be between two lines of latitude
   or between two lines of longitude?

   _____

8. Do the lines of longitude on a political map go from east to west

   or from north to south? _____

Dictionary

📖 Use Handbook pages 250–251.

■ **Read the questions.**

■ **Use the dictionary pages in your Handbook to answer the questions.**

1. What is a dictionary?

   a book filled with information about words _____

2. How are the words in a dictionary organized?

   _____

3. Would you find the word *gravity* in the front, middle, or back part

   of a dictionary? _____

4. In which part of a dictionary would you find the word *orbit*?

   _____

5. What do the guide words on each dictionary page tell you?

   _____

6. Look at the guide words on page 250. Which word comes last

   on the dictionary page? _____

7. Does the entry for *spacewalk* come before or after *spacecraft*? _____

8. Look at the guide words on page 251. Why is the word *spamming*
   on this page?

   _____

9. Which two entry words is the word *spamming* between?

   _____

10. Would the guide words on the page that comes <u>after</u> the one on page 251

    be **sourball • South Pole** or **Spanish • speak**? _____

Dictionary

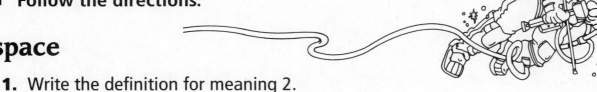

📖 **Use Handbook pages 252–253.**

■ **Look at the dictionary pages in your Handbook. Find the entry for each word.**

■ **Follow the directions.**

space

1. Write the definition for meaning 2.

_____

2. Write a sentence using meaning 4.

_____

_____

3. Tell the word's part of speech. _____

4. Write the plural form of the word used as a noun. _____

5. Show how to pronounce the singular form of the word. _____

spacesuit

6. Write the definition.

_____

_____

7. Write a sentence using the meaning.

_____

_____

8. Tell the word's part of speech. _____

9. Write the plural form of the word. _____

10. Show how to pronounce the singular form of the word. _____

Encyclopedia

📖 Use Handbook pages 254–255.

■ **Read each question.**

■ **Fill in the circle for the correct answer.**

1. What is each book in an encyclopedia called?
   ● volume   ○ article   ○ topic

2. What does each volume in an encyclopedia contain?
   ○ stories   ○ articles   ○ questions

3. What is the last volume in a set of encyclopedias called?
   ○ index   ○ dictionary   ○ almanac

4. In which order would these articles appear in volume 1?
   ○ asteroid, atom,   ○ aircraft, asteroid,   ○ aircraft, atom,
      aircraft   atom   asteroid

5. Which volume would have an article about Mars?
   ○ volume 1   ○ volume 13   ○ volume 21

6. What are the words at the top of each page called?
   ○ guide words   ○ headings   ○ entry words

7. What is the title of an article called?
   ○ a guide word   ○ the heading   ○ an entry word

8. What is the title of each section of an article called?
   ○ a guide word   ○ the heading   ○ an entry word

9. What is the entry word for the article on **Handbook** page 255?
   ○ Mars   ○ orbit and rotation   ○ Mars at a glance

10. What is the article on **Handbook** page 255 mostly about?
    ○ space missions   ○ size, orbit, and   ○ the solar system
                                   location of Mars

Name _____ Date _____

Telephone Directory

📖 Use Handbook pages 256–257.

■ Pretend that you are planning a party.

■ Write a list of the businesses you would call and their phone numbers. Write the list in alphabetical order.

PAPADATOS—PATRICK

Papadatos Demetrios. 622-8252
Papa Joe's Party Supplies 622-1898
Pappas Lambros 622-8400
Pardo Jeanna. 622-2623
Paredes Ignacio 622-7751
Park Jin Ki 622-0003
Parkway Little League 622-8002
Parna M 622-8989
Party Central 622-5545
PARTY TIME
  111 Centre St. 622-0189
Party Works 622-4587

Party—Patio 567

Party Supplies—Retail and Rental

AA Rentals
"Everything You Need"
Tables • Chairs • China • Linen • Games • Decorations
125 Greenwood 622-8909

Balloons for You 622-9475

Party Time
  Party Supplies • Tents
  111 Centre St 622-0189

AA Rentals, 622-8909
_____

_____

_____

_____

_____

■ Is there anything else you need for your party? Write some other guide words you would use to look up businesses in the yellow pages.

_____   _____

_____   _____

Name _____   Date _____

Drafting

📖 Use Handbook page 88.

- **Tell how to make a mask.**

- **Write the directions. Be sure to include the materials you need and to put the steps in order.**

What kind of mask is it?

_____

What materials do you need to make the mask?

_____   _____

_____   _____

_____   _____

What are the steps for making the mask?
What should someone do to make it?

1. _____

_____

2. _____

_____

3. _____

_____

4. _____

_____

5. _____

_____

Name _____ Date _____

Revising

📖 Use Handbook pages 89–91.

**Revise these directions. Be sure the steps
are clear and are in the correct order.**

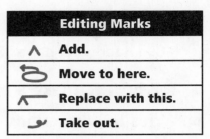

How to Make a Headband

You'll need: paper   stickers   glue   ruler
                glitter   scissors

3 inches

Second, cut 1 strip of paper the same length as the string.

First, use the string to measure your head. Make the strip

inches wide. Decorate the strip with stickers. Fourth, the ends

of the strip together. The glue dries. Put on your headband.

Proofreading

📖 Use Handbook page 92.

**Proofread these directions.
Be sure to use commands
and add any missing commas.**

How to Make a Halloween Mask

You'll need: paper plate   paper scraps   scissors   string
                yarn   glue   markers

1. The paper plate goes up to your face. Have someone

   mark your eyes nose and mouth.

2. Put the plate down Then the holes.

Decorate the plate with paper scraps markers or yarn.

4. poke a hole on each side and attach the strng.

5. The mask is for halloween.

Drafting

📖 **Use Handbook page 88.**

- **Write about the first time you did something.**

- **Use lots of details to tell when it happened,
  what it was like, and how you felt.**

The first time I _____

was _____

_____.

It was _____

_____.

⬇

At first, when I _____

_____

_____.

Then, _____

_____.

⬇

Finally, _____

_____

_____.

I felt _____

_____.

Revising

📖 Use Handbook pages 89–91.

Revise this personal narrative. Be sure to add details to give a good picture of what happened.

Editing Marks	
∧	Add.
⤺	Move to here.
⤶	Replace with this.
⤴	Take out.

On my birthday, I went bowling for the first time.

I had to use both hands to pick up that ball!

Then I tried to roll the ball down the alley.

The third time, I did it! The first time, I dropped

the ball behind. The second time, it went into

the gutter! The ball rolled in a line toward the pins.

Finally, I knocked pins down! Now I like to bowl!

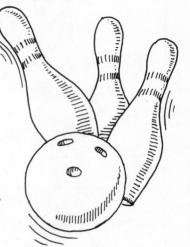

Proofreading

📖 Use Handbook page 92.

Proofread this personal narrative. Be sure to use pronouns correctly.

Proofreading Marks			
∧	Add.	⬭	Check spelling.
⩟	Add a comma.	╱	Make lowercase.
⊙	Add a period.	¶	Start a new paragraph.
☰	Capitalize.	⤴	Take out.

Last year, I won the school Spelling Bee. They wasn't easy

to win mrs. Lee gave we hard words to spell like *receive* and

occasion. He is our principal Mom had helped I practice, so i spelled

all the words correctly. i was really proud of yourself.

Drafting

📖 Use Handbook page 88.

- **What news do you want to share with someone you know? What do you want to ask the person?**

- **Write a friendly letter.**

_____

_____

_____ , _____

Dear _____ ,

    I've got news for you!_____

_____

_____

    How are you?_____

_____

_____

_____

_____

_____

Revising

📖 Use Handbook pages 89–91.

Revise this part of a friendly letter. Be sure to use questions so Elinor will write back.

Editing Marks	
∧	Add.
⤴	Move to here.
⌐	Replace with this.
⤲	Take out.

Elinor,

    We're coming to New York City in the May. I don't no what

to pack. It might be warm or cool in May. I can't wait to see you!

                          Sami

Proofreading

📖 Use Handbook page 92.

Proofread this friendly letter. Be sure to use capital letters and punctuation correctly.

Proofreading Marks			
∧	Add.	◯	Check spelling.
⋏	Add a comma.	/	Make lowercase.
⊙	Add a period.	¶	Start a new paragraph.
≡	Capitalize.	⤲	Take out.

                  2435 oak Street

                  San Jose, ca 95110

                  january 10 2001

Dear Keiko

    My family is getting ready for Kwanzaa. That's when we

celebrate our african ancestry and spend lots of time together.

What's your favorite holiday in japan

                  Your friend

                  Yolanda

Drafting

📖 Use Handbook page 88.

- **What is important to you? What do you want changed? What should someone do to change it?**

- **Write a persuasive paragraph.**

1. Tell your opinion or how you feel about something.

I think that the _____

should _____

_____

_____ .

2. Give reasons for your opinion. Tell why you want something changed.

It is important to _____

because _____

_____

_____

_____

_____

_____ .

3. Tell what you want someone to do.

Please _____

_____

_____

_____ .

Revising

📖 Use Handbook pages 89–91.

Revise this persuasive paragraph. Be sure to add persuasive words and reasons for the opinion.

Editing Marks	
∧	Add.
⟳	Move to here.
⟍	Replace with this.
⤴	Take out.

    We can only check out two books at a time. I think that the library rule for checking out books is unfair. This is a problem because we have to keep coming back to get more. Also, we like to find lots of facts for our research reports. Here's another reason. Reading more books helps students. We would like to change this rule. Ask the librarian to let us check out more books at a time!

Proofreading

📖 Use Handbook page 92.

Proofread this persuasive paragraph. Be sure to add helping verbs where they are needed.

Proofreading Marks			
∧	Add.	⬭	Check spelling.
⏥	Add a comma.	/	Make lowercase.
⊙	Add a period.	¶	Start a new paragraph.
≡	Capitalize.	⤴	Take out.

    I feel that our class not have enough computers Right now, there are only three computers, and everyone is in line to use them. The computers run old, too. Every student have a chance to use a computter when he or she needs to. If we had more and newer computers, all of us do our best work. we finish our reports on time, too!

Drafting

📖 Use Handbook page 88.

- Draw a picture of your favorite place, animal, season, or food.

- Write a poem to tell what it is like.

```




```

_____
Title

1. _____
Topic

2. _____
Words That Tell What the Topic Is Like

3. _____
More Words That Tell What the Topic Is Like

4. _____
More Words That Tell What the Topic Is Like

5. _____
Topic

Revising

📖 Use Handbook pages 89–91.

Revise this poem. Be sure the details give a good picture of the topic.

Editing Marks	
∧	Add.
∽	Move to here.
⌅	Replace with this.
∽	Take out.

City Senses

See the buildings and the bridges.

Smell the food coming from the restaurant.

Listen to the cars passing along on the street.

This is where I live.

Proofreading

📖 Use Handbook page 92.

Proofread this poem. Be sure to spell plural nouns correctly.

Proofreading Marks			
∧	Add.	◯	Check spelling.
⋏	Add a comma.	/	Make lowercase.
⊙	Add a period.	¶	Start a new paragraph.
≡	Capitalize.	∽	Take out.

Two Pizzas

pizzas   Pizzas

Steaming slice   Order them now

Two kind of melted cheese   The child are hungry

Pepperoni, no anchovy   They'll them right from the box

Pizza   Pizzas

Drafting

📖 Use Handbook page 88.

■ **Make up some characters and a setting that are like people and places you know.**

■ **Write a story. Tell about events that could happen in real life.**

1. Name the characters. Tell about the place and time.

_____ and _____

were at the _____

_____ .

It was _____

_____

2. Tell what the problem is.

_____

_____ , but _____

_____

_____ .

3. Tell what happens. What do the characters say and do?

_____

_____

_____

_____

_____

4. Tell what finally happens. Tell how the problem is solved.

_____

so _____

_____ .

Revising

📖 Use Handbook pages 89–91.

Revise this story. Be sure the details and dialogue seem like real life.

Editing Marks	
∧	Add.
↻	Move to here.
↰	Replace with this.
⤴	Take out.

"Good morning, Ryan," said Grandma. "Your face looks sad to me. What's wrong?"

"I have a nervous feeling about the volleyball game. When it's my turn to serve, I can't hit the ball over."

"Why, I was a champ when I was younger," Grandma said. "Come on."

Proofreading

📖 Use Handbook page 92.

Proofread this story. Be sure to use quotation marks and contractions correctly.

Proofreading Marks			
∧	Add.	◯	Check spelling.
⩕	Add a comma.	／	Make lowercase.
⊙	Add a period.	¶	Start a new paragraph.
≡	Capitalize.	⤴	Take out.

Carlo Mendicino wasn't looking forward to summer vacation.

I don't want school to be over, he told his mom. "Im really going to miss my art class. When carlo got home from school, his mom said "I have a big surprise. Ive enrolled you in art school this Summer.

"Thats great, Mom. Thanks. Now it'll be a great summer."

Drafting

📖 Use Handbook page 88.

■ Write about something that happened to you on a special day.

■ Use lots of details to tell when something happened, what things were like, and how you felt.

On _____, _____

_____

_____

_____

_____

↓

Then, _____

_____

_____

_____

_____

↓

Finally, _____

_____

_____

_____

_____

Revising

📖 Use Handbook pages 89–91.

Revise this personal narrative. Be sure the details give a good picture of what happened.

Editing Marks	
∧	Add.
∿	Move to here.
⌐	Replace with this.
⤶	Take out.

On Thanksgiving Day, my family went to my aunt's house who is my mom's sister. I could smell the food, but we had to wait to eat. My stomach was making noises. Then, it was time to eat. I piled mashed potatoes, turkey, gravy, cranberries, and stuffing on my plate. It tasted good. Finally, I took a bite.

Proofreading

📖 Use Handbook page 92.

Proofread this personal narrative. Be sure to use pronouns correctly.

Proofreading Marks			
∧	Add.	◯	Check spelling.
⋏	Add a comma.	╱	Make lowercase.
⊙	Add a period.	¶	Start a new paragraph.
≡	Capitalize.	⤶	Take out.

Dad bought a piñata. She bought it for my birthday party. The piñata looked like a swan. It's beak was orange and its feathers were white My friend and me took turns hitting the piñata while my Dad pulled it up and down. Then when i hit the piñata, they broke open. Finally, us got lots of candy!

Drafting

📖 Use Handbook page 88.

■ Write about your classmate.

■ Use lots of details to tell what that person looks like and likes to do. Tell how that person is special.

Guess Who?

This person has _____ eyes and _____ hair and is _____.

I like the way my classmate _____

_____.

and _____

_____.

This mystery person loves to _____

_____.

My classmate is also very good at _____

_____.

I know this because _____

_____.

The most surprising thing about this person is _____

_____

_____.

Can you guess who this person is?

Revising

📖 Use Handbook pages 89–91.

- **Look at the boy on Handbook pages 18–19.**
- **Then revise this character sketch. Be sure the details and examples give a good picture of what the boy is like.**

The boy is about five feet tall and has blond hair and eyes.

He really likes sports, and is a good player.

This boy loves to write. He often writes down stories his family

tells. He has a lot of relatives. Sometimes at school he stays inside

so he can write stories.

Proofreading

📖 Use Handbook page 92.

Proofread this paragraph. Be sure each subject agrees with its verb.

My friend has emerald green eyes and a beautiful smile

She are a very happy person. she is also the friendlyest person

I knows.

She like to play with her dog Sundae. He have a White belly,

Yellow sides, and Brown back. My friend's brothers thinks that

the dog looks like an ice cream sundae!

Drafting

📖 Use Handbook page 88.

- ■ **Write a tall tale.**
- ■ **Use lots of details to make your character and the events unbelievable!**

1. Draw a picture of your tall tale character.

2. Tell what your character wants.

_____ wants to

_____ because _____

_____ .

3. Tell what the character does to get what he or she wants.

So one day _____

_____

_____ .

Next, _____

_____

_____ .

Then, _____

_____

_____ .

4. Tell what happens in the end. Does your character get what he or she wants?

Finally, _____

_____

_____

_____ .

Revising

📖 Use Handbook pages 89–91.

Revise this tall tale. Be sure to use synonyms to make the story entertaining and impossible to believe.

Editing Marks	
∧	Add.
↶	Move to here.
⌐	Replace with this.
✐	Take out.

    Tiny Jack was little, but he was strong. Once he went into an ant hole in Kentucky. No one saw him for three days. He said that he had built a children's playground. When he finally came home. When the children went into the hole, they found a big cave! It was the cave, Mammoth-Flint Ridge Cave, which is over 190 miles long!

Proofreading

📖 Use Handbook page 92.

Proofread this tall tale. Look for short sentences that can be combined with a comma and *and, but,* or *or.*

Proofreading Marks			
∧	Add.	◯	Check spelling.
⋏	Add a comma.	/	Make lowercase.
⊙	Add a period.	¶	Start a new paragraph.
≡	Capitalize.	✐	Take out.

    Go to Arizona. You'll see the Painted Desert. Why is it called that Well, Fine Fran loved the desert. She hated all the yellow dirt. She could leave Arizona. She could change the desert's color. Then she had an idea. Fran pulled a rainbow down from the sky. Then she swept it across the land. She painted the dessert with all the colors of the rainbow

Drafting

📖 Use Handbook page 88.

■ **Write a business letter. Ask someone for the things you need to do your class project.**

_____

_____

_____

(Your address and the date.)

_____

_____

_____

(Address of the business or company.)

Dear _____ :

I am a student at _____

_____ . Our class is doing a project to improve our school.

We want to _____

_____ .

Can you donate _____

or _____ ?

Thank you very much for your help.

Sincerely yours,

_____

(Your signature.)

_____

(Your name printed.)

Revising

📖 Use Handbook pages 89–91.

Revise the body of this business letter. Be sure to use formal language and make the request clear.

Editing Marks	
∧	Add.
↰	Move to here.
⌐	Replace with this.
✌	Take out.

Our class wants to beautify River School. We are gonna start

planting some flowers and stuff like that in front of the school.

I want you to send us something. We'll also need some tools.

Thanks.

Proofreading

📖 Use Handbook page 92.

Proofread this business letter. Use capital letters and punctuation correctly.

Proofreading Marks			
∧	Add.	⬭	Check spelling.
⋏	Add a comma.	/	Make lowercase.
⊙	Add a period.	¶	Start a new paragraph.
≡	Capitalize.	✌	Take out.

492 Washington ave.

Chicago IL 60001

september 3, 2000

Zeke's Hardware

562 willow St.

Chicago, il 60001

Dear sir or Madam

Our class is cleaning up the trash around Parkview School. Can

Zeke's hardware donate some trash bags We appreciate your help,

Sincerely yours

Kathy Alcantara

Kathy Alcantara

Drafting

📖 Use Handbook page 88.

- **Write an advertisement for the Class Newspaper.**
- **Follow the steps below.**

Muffins for Sale

Huge, yummy, fresh chocolate chip and blueberry muffins. $1.00 each.

Order from Jessica in Ms. Fernandez's room (Rm. 9). Next day delivery.

1. Draw a picture of what you want to buy, sell, or trade.

2. Name the item. Tell what it is like. Tell how much it costs.

3. Tell what people should do to find out about the item.

Revising

📖 Use Handbook pages 89–91.

Revise this editorial. Be sure to add important details and facts.

Editing Marks	
∧	Add.
⟲	Move to here.
⌐	Replace with this.
⤳	Take out.

Fifth Grade Needs Playground Equipment

We think that kids at Jefferson Elementary School need new

equipment. Most of the ones have popped. The jump ropes are old.

We like to play baseball, but we need things. Please talk to anyone

you can. Ask them to help us get what we want.

Proofreading

📖 Use Handbook page 92.

Proofread this news story. Be sure to use nouns correctly.

Proofreading Marks			
∧	Add.	⬭	Check spelling.
⋀	Add a comma.	/	Make lowercase.
⊙	Add a period.	¶	Start a new paragraph.
≡	Capitalize.	⤳	Take out.

Finley project Helps Neighbors

LAREDO, Texas—cata Ortíz was just one of the child from

finley Elementary School who participated in Make-a-Difference Day.

On october 25, several volunteers and laredo Rotary member

gave clothing to 35 familys who were victims of the recent floods.

"We were happy to help," said 11-year-old ortíz. "We hope that we

can get more person involved next Year."

Drafting

📖 Use Handbook page 88.

■ **Look at your outline. Use the title, main ideas, and details to write a report.**

Title: _____

Interesting
Introduction: _____
_____
_____
_____ .

Topic Sentence
for Main Idea I: _____
_____ .

Detail Sentences: _____
_____
_____
_____ .

Topic Sentence
for Main Idea II: _____
_____ .

Detail Sentences: _____
_____
_____
_____ .

Conclusion That
Tells Each Main
Idea: _____
_____
_____
_____ .

Revising

📖 Use Handbook pages 88–91.

Revise these paragraphs from a report. Be sure each paragraph has a topic sentence.

Editing Marks	
∧	Add.
↰	Move to here.
⌐	Replace with this.
⤶	Take out.

I. Life on Saturn and Jupiter
A. Probably none on Saturn
B. Maybe tiny organisms on Jupiter
II. Rings around Saturn and Jupiter different
A. Saturn has 7 big rings made of ice
B. Jupiter has 1 thin ring made of rock

Some scientists don't believe that there are plants or animals on Saturn. However, it's possible that organisms do exist on Jupiter.

Saturn has rings than Jupiter. Both Saturn and Jupiter have rings, but the rings are different. It has seven big rings made of ice. Neptune has rings. Jupiter has only won thin ring made of rock.

Proofreading

📖 Use Handbook page 92.

Proofread this paragraph. Be sure the correct adjectives are used to compare things.

Proofreading Marks			
∧	Add.	⬯	Check spelling.
⋏	Add a comma.	/	Make lowercase.
⊙	Add a period.	¶	Start a new paragraph.
≡	Capitalize.	⤶	Take out.

The Big Dipper and Little Dipper are groups of stars that look like ladles. Each group has seven stars, but the Big Dipper is bright than the Little Dipper. It's also big. however, the Little Dipper is most important for showing which way is north The more visible star in that group is the North Star, which is almost over the North Pole?

Drafting

📖 Use Handbook page 88.

- **Look at your diagram. Use it to help you think about what your place is like.**

- **Write a description of the place. Be sure to use direction words like *right, left, next to, close to, above,* or *below* to tell where things are.**

_____
(Name of Place)

The _____ in _____

is _____ .

When you go there, the first thing you'll see _____

_____

_____ .

If you look _____ you'll see _____

_____

_____

_____ to that you'll see _____

_____

_____

_____ .

Finally, look _____ and you'll see

_____

_____ .

Revising

📖 Use Handbook pages 89–91.

Revise this description. Use lots of details to
help the readers imagine that they are there!

I like to sit on a bench in the park.

There are two trees filled with birds.

There's a pond where some ducks splash and

play. I sit there so the ducks won't notice

me. In the summer sun, the water sparkles.

Proofreading

📖 Use Handbook page 92.

Proofread this description.
Use the correct adjectives
to make comparisons. Use
the correct prepositions.

There are four theaters in town, but the Galaxy is the

nicer. It's old than the City cinema. After you walk inside

its glass doors, you'll see the colorful carpet anywhere As

you look beside the lobby, you'll see huge posters near

famous movy stars. Don't forget to look up to see the more

beautiful crystal chandeliers hanging the ceiling.

Drafting

📖 Use Handbook page 88.

- **What did you discover about something at school? Write a useful tip for a new student that tells what you learned.**

- **Then write a personal narrative to tell how you made the discovery. Use details that tell when, where, and what happened.**

TIP: _____

_____

This is how I found out:

Last _____,

I was _____

when _____

_____.

First I _____

_____

_____.

Then I _____

_____.

That's when I learned that _____

_____

_____

_____.

Name _____ Date _____

Revising

📖 Use Handbook pages 89–91.

Revise this personal narrative. Be sure the details give a good picture of what happened.

TIP: Ask Mrs. Mitchell to help you find something good to read!

I hated going to the school library. I sat in a chair and waited

until it was time to leave. Then I asked Mrs. Mitchell, the

librarian, if there were any books. I like horses. She showed me

books about ponies, stallions, and colorful pintos. I'm never

nervous or bored at the library now.

Proofreading

📖 Use Handbook page 92.

Proofread this personal narrative. Be sure to use pronouns correctly.

TIP: Try after-school basketball!

I used to walk home right after school with my sister, Maya.

Her and I didn't know there were things to do after school. Then

one day i heard some kids talk about playing Basketball after school.

so that day, we stayed to see for themselves The kids asked us to

play with they! Maya and i didn't know how to play basketball but

our new friends taught we.

Name _____ Date _____

Drafting

📖 **Use Handbook page 88.**

■ **Look at your KWL chart.**

■ **Use the details and facts to write sentences and paragraphs for a biography.**

Our Guest: _____

1. Name the person. Tell when and where he or she was born.

_____

_____

_____

_____

2. Tell how the person learned his or her job.

_____

_____

_____

_____

_____

_____

_____

3. Tell what the person does now or what his or her job is like.

_____

_____

_____

_____

_____

_____

_____

Revising

📖 Use Handbook pages 89–91.

Revise this biography. Use the chart to check the facts. Be sure to add sequence words.

Editing Marks	
∧	Add.
↶	Move to here.
↖	Replace with this.
⤶	Take out.

```
          L
What I Learned

• Born in Italy, 1952.
• Went to New York at 18.
• Was a waiter, then
  a cook.
• Bought a restaurant
  at 30.
  Named it
  "Nana's Kitchen."
```

When he was 18 he moved to New York. Roy Giacone was born in Spain in 1952. He worked in a small restaurant in the city as a waiter. He became a cook. He bought his own restaurant when he was 20. Roy named it "The Kitchen" after his grandmother.

Proofreading

📖 Use Handbook page 92.

Proofread this biography. Be sure the verbs are in the correct tense.

Proofreading Marks			
∧	Add.	⌒	Check spelling.
⋏	Add a comma.	/	Make lowercase.
⊙	Add a period.	¶	Start a new paragraph.
≡	Capitalize.	⤶	Take out.

Tamara Lewis is born in 1958 in California. As a young girl, Tamara loves to study plants, boogs, and animals. After high school, Tamara goes to the University of washington to study biology. After she graduated, Tamara becomes a biologist For a company called Bio Gene

Drafting

📖 Use Handbook page 88.

■ **What do you want changed? Write a business letter to tell how you feel about it and what you want someone to do.**

_____

_____

_____
(Your address and the date.)

_____

_____

_____
(Address of the business or group.)

Dear Sir or Madam:

I think that _____

_____.

I think this way because _____

_____.

Also, _____

_____

_____.

Please _____

_____

_____.

Sincerely,

_____
(Your signature.)

_____
(Your name printed.)

Name _____ Date _____

Revising

📖 Use Handbook pages 89–91.

Revise this paragraph from a persuasive business letter. Be sure to use persuasive words.

Editing Marks	
∧	Add.
∽	Move to here.
⌐	Replace with this.
⌙	Take out.

I think the school needs to buy some computers for our class.
It's good for us to learn how to use them! We want computers so we
can do research and write reports. Order some computers for us.

Proofreading

📖 Use Handbook page 92.

Proofread this letter.
Use capital letters and punctuation correctly.

Proofreading Marks			
∧ Add.		⬯ Check spelling.	
⩍ Add a comma.		/ Make lowercase.	
⊙ Add a period.		¶ Start a new paragraph.	
≡ Capitalize.		⌙ Take out.	

4937 Rancho st.
Barstow, CA 98773
April 27 2000

City Council
22001 S. Sunset St.
Barstow, Ca 98773

dear Mrs. Ruíz

I feel that we need a new city park. now kids are playing in
the street. That's very dangerous Please tell the city Council that
we must have a safe place to play.

With best regards
Nicholas Benton
Nicholas Benton

Drafting

📖 Use Handbook page 88.

- Look at your story map.

- Use the details to write a story about an event in history. Make your characters act, talk, and dress like people who lived during that time.

Title: _____

1. Tell when and where the event happened and who was there.

The year was _____. _____ and _____ were at the _____ _____ in _____ .

2. Tell what your characters did and said.

_____

_____

_____

_____

_____

_____ .

_____

_____

_____

_____ .

_____

_____ .

3. Tell what finally happened.

_____

_____

_____

_____ .

Revising

📖 Use Handbook pages 89–91.

Revise this story. Be sure the details tell
about the past.

Editing Marks	
∧	Add.
↶	Move to here.
↖	Replace with this.
⌇	Take out.

The first Thanksgiving feast was about to begin at the

restaurant. Mother was cooking a wild bird called a turkey in the

oven and fixing some frozen corn-on-the-cob. We were getting out

the China bowls and plates.

"We wouldn't have all this food if the Wampanoag hadn't helped

us the winter. They taught us how to do things," said Mother.

Proofreading

📖 Use Handbook page 92.

Proofread this story. Be sure
to use nouns and punctuation
in the dialogue correctly.

Proofreading Marks			
∧	Add.	⬭	Check spelling.
⩔	Add a comma.	/	Make lowercase.
⊙	Add a period.	¶	Start a new paragraph.
≡	Capitalize.	⌇	Take out.

"What are you doing up there? asked Robert Smith. He was

watching several man throwing thing off a ship in Boston Harbor.

We're protesting the unfair tax on tea" they said. Maybe the

British will listen to us if we dump these box of tea into the

harbor. "You are very brave to protest like this for our

independence" said Robert. "May I join you?"

Name _____ Date _____

Drafting
📖 Use Handbook page 88.

- Look at the notes you took during your interview.
- Write a report to share what you learned.

An Interview with _____

by _____

Why did you decide to volunteer?

Q: _____ ?

A: _____

_____

_____ .

Q: _____ ?

A: _____

_____

_____ .

Q: _____ ?

A: _____

_____

_____ .

Q: _____ ?

A: _____

_____

_____ .

Revising

📖 Use Handbook pages 89–91.

Revise this report from an interview.
Be sure the details are correct.

Editing Marks	
∧	Add.
↺	Move to here.
⅄	Replace with this.
⸜	Take out.

Questions to Ask Derek Johnson

What do you do at the Midtown Food Bank?

Well, I pick up donated canned goods from grocery stores. Then I take the food to people who need it.

How many hours do you volunteer?

I'm usually busy about 4 hours every Saturday. Every minute is worth it, though. I love helping people.

An Interview

Q: What do you do at the Food Bank?

A: I buy canned goods from grocery stores.

Then I take the food to people who need it.

Q: How many hours do you volunteer?

A: He's usually busy about 2 hours every

Saturday. Every minute is worth it, though.

I love people. Especially the people I work for.

Proofreading

📖 Use Handbook page 92.

Proofread this part of a report from an interview. Fix the mistakes in punctuation and verb tense.

Proofreading Marks			
∧	Add.	⬭	Check spelling.
⅄	Add a comma.	/	Make lowercase.
⊙	Add a period.	¶	Start a new paragraph.
≡	Capitalize.	⸜	Take out.

Diane Hollis volunteered a few hours every week at the Humane

Society? I asked her, "Why do you volunteer " Diane said, I love

animals and it made me sad to see them so lonely. Animals always

liked getting lots of attention.

ENGLISH
At Your Command!

Student
Progress
Test

Vocabulary

Mark the answer that means about the same thing as the underlined part. The sample has been done for you.

Sample

The lifeguard was <u>concerned</u> about the big waves.
- ○ amused
- ○ surprised
- ○ interested
- ● worried

---

1 Did the missing cat <u>turn up</u> yet?
- ○ appear
- ○ look up
- ○ run away
- ○ turn over

2 She will <u>look over</u> the homework tomorrow.
- ○ copy
- ○ pick up
- ○ review
- ○ turn in

3 The boys <u>spilled the beans about the party</u>.
- ○ ate a meal at the party
- ○ cooked beans for the party
- ○ made a mess at the party
- ○ told people the party was happening

4 I always <u>hit the books</u> before a test.
- ○ eat
- ○ go to bed early
- ○ go to the library
- ○ study

5 Junji found some <u>inexpensive</u> toys at the yard sale.
- ○ broken
- ○ cheap
- ○ costly
- ○ special

6 The musicians sat in a <u>semicircle</u>.
- ○ big circle
- ○ half circle
- ○ pair of circles
- ○ ring of circles

7 The path went <u>upward</u>.
- ○ to the bottom
- ○ to the inside
- ○ to the middle
- ○ to the top

8 Some people <u>weep</u> at the movies.
- ○ cry
- ○ eat
- ○ laugh
- ○ sleep

9 The statue had been buried for <u>a century</u>.
- ○ one hundred years
- ○ one thousand years
- ○ ten years
- ○ twenty years

GO ON ➡

10 Recess ends at <u>quarter past</u> ten.
- ○ nine forty-five
- ○ nine thirty
- ○ ten fifteen
- ○ ten twenty-five

11 The sky looks lovely at <u>dusk</u>.
- ○ daybreak
- ○ midnight
- ○ noon
- ○ sunset

12 I go to the dentist <u>semiannually</u>.
- ○ every two years
- ○ monthly
- ○ two times in a year
- ○ yearly

13 We go hiking when the weather is <u>fair</u>.
- ○ clear and sunny
- ○ good for rides and games
- ○ the same for all

14 The <u>bat</u> cracked when she hit a home run.
- ○ long wooden stick
- ○ small flying animal
- ○ small round ball

15 My <u>ring</u> has a shiny green stone.
- ○ jingling phone
- ○ large circle
- ○ piece of jewelry

Mark the answer that best completes the sentence.

16 The sail on this boat is shaped like _____.
- ○ a diamond
- ○ a rectangle
- ○ a triangle
- ○ an oval

17 The _____ sock has stripes on it.
- ○ fifth
- ○ five
- ○ fifty
- ○ fourth

18 The mouse is _____ the pumpkins.
- ○ behind
- ○ between
- ○ below
- ○ inside

19 It's hard to _____ on a foggy night.
- ○ sea
- ○ see

20 Let's take the road _____ town.
- ○ threw
- ○ through

STOP

Organizing Ideas

Read each item and mark your answer. The sample has been done for you.

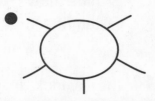
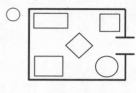

Sample

Which of these would you use to make a word web?

○   ○   ●

---

1 Look at this diagram. It is most useful for showing

○ four steps in a process

○ how details are related to the main idea

○ the ways in which two things are alike

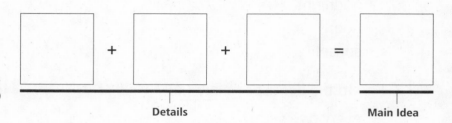

Details   Main Idea

---

2 Which of these would <u>not</u> be used to show the sequence of events?

○   ○   ○

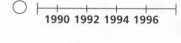

1990 1992 1994 1996

---

3 Which of these would you use to show how a bird and a turtle are alike and different?

○   ○   ○

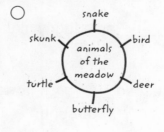
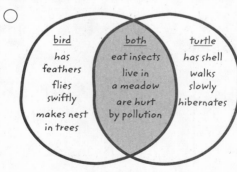
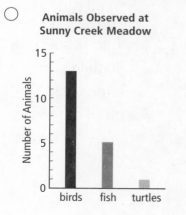

Animals Observed at Sunny Creek Meadow

Read the paragraph. Then, find the graphic organizer that best shows what the paragraph is about.

Alvar Nuñez Cabeza De Vaca was born in southern Spain in 1490. Like his grandfathers, Alvar became a soldier and was soon known for his bravery. In 1527, the King of Spain sent him to explore Florida, in North America. The trip was a disaster: all but four of the men died. But Cabeza de Vaca did not give up. He led the other three men on a walk across the unfamiliar land. That journey lasted eight years and covered hundreds of miles!

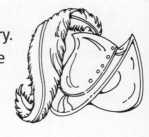

4

To make dipped wax candles, first, melt some wax in a tall tin can set in a pot of water on a stove. While the wax melts, cut wicks to the length you want. To make your candle, dip the wick into the melted wax and pull it out. Dip the wick into a can of cold water to cool it. Continue dipping into the hot wax and then into the cold water until there is enough wax built up to make a candle that's as thick as you want. Be sure to work with a grown-up, because hot wax is dangerous!

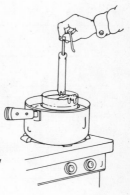

5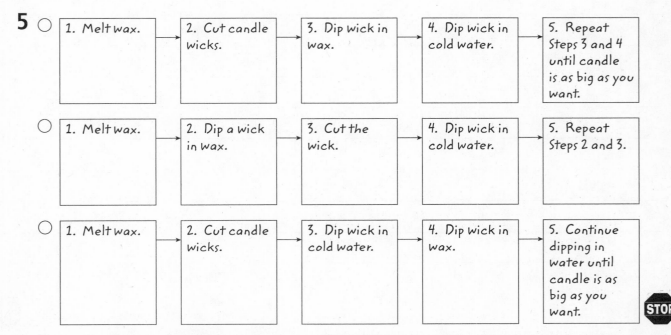

○ 1. Melt wax. → 2. Cut candle wicks. → 3. Dip wick in wax. → 4. Dip wick in cold water. → 5. Repeat Steps 3 and 4 until candle is as big as you want.

○ 1. Melt wax. → 2. Dip a wick in wax. → 3. Cut the wick. → 4. Dip wick in cold water. → 5. Repeat Steps 2 and 3.

○ 1. Melt wax. → 2. Cut candle wicks. → 3. Dip wick in cold water. → 4. Dip wick in wax. → 5. Continue dipping in water until candle is as big as you want.

STOP

Writing

Choose a season of the year. Think about what it is like and what people do during that time of year. Write a description of that season. Be sure to include colorful verbs and words that describe in your writing.

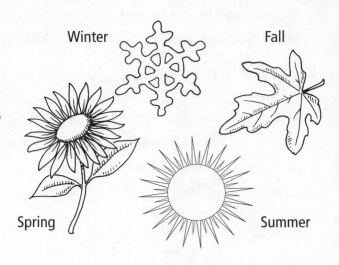

Winter

Fall

Spring

Summer

_____

_____

_____

_____

_____

_____

_____

_____

_____

_____

_____

_____

_____

_____

_____

_____

_____

_____

Think of a gift you have received, or imagine one you would like to get. Write a thank-you note to say "thank you" for the gift. In addition to expressing your thanks in the body of the letter, be sure to also include the date, greeting, and closing in your letter.

_____

_____

_____

_____

_____

_____

_____

_____

_____

_____

_____

_____

                        _____

                        _____

STOP

Language

Read each paragraph. Then, read the question about each underlined part and mark your answer. The sample has been done for you.

Sample

<u>The armadillo are an interesting animal.</u> The female always has four babies, and
             _S

they are either all boys or all girls!

S Which of these is the best way to write Part S?
  - ○ Armadillos is an interesting animal.
  - ● The armadillo is an interesting animal.
  - ○ Best as it is.

You may have heard of <u>Lewis and Clark, and did you ever hear</u> of Sacagawea?
                    ₁

She was <u>a young Shoshone mother who helped Lewis and Clark</u> on their Expedition.
                 ₂

<u>Sacagawea helping to get horses</u> from the Shoshone people. <u>Without no horses,</u>
         ₃   ₄

the Expedition could not cross the Rocky Mountains.

---

1 Which of these is the best way to write Part 1?
  - ○ Lewis and Clark, but did you ever hear
  - ○ Lewis and Clark, so did you ever hear
  - ○ Lewis and Clark. Did you ever hear
  - ○ Best as it is.

2 Which of these is the best way to write Part 2?
  - ○ a young Shoshone mother what helped Lewis and Clark
  - ○ a young Shoshone mother which helped Lewis and Clark
  - ○ a young Shoshone mother. She helped Lewis and Clark
  - ○ Best as it is.

3 Which of these is the best way to write Part 3?
  - ○ Sacagawea helped to get horses
  - ○ Sacagawea helps to get horses
  - ○ Sacagawea been helping to get horses
  - ○ Best as it is.

4 Which of these is the best way to write Part 4?
  - ○ Not with any horses,
  - ○ With any horses,
  - ○ Without any horses,
  - ○ Best as it is.

The word *zero* means "nothing." You or I both know that. But do you know where the zero was first used? The Mayans was probably the first people to use the zero, around the year 300. Several hundred years later, the zero begin to be used in India.

5 Which of these is the best way to write Part 5?
- ○ The word *zero*.
- ○ The word *zero* means.
- ○ Means "nothing."
- ○ Best as it is.

6 Which of these is the best way to write Part 6?
- ○ You and I both know that.
- ○ You and me both know that.
- ○ I or you both know that.
- ○ Best as it is.

7 Which of these is the best way to write Part 7?
- ○ The Mayans is probably the first people
- ○ The Mayans were probably the first people
- ○ The Mayans will probably be the first people
- ○ Best as it is.

8 Which of these is the best way to write Part 8?
- ○ later, the zero began to be used
- ○ later, the zero begins to be used
- ○ later, the zero beginning to be used
- ○ Best as it is.

Mark the answer that best completes each sentence.

9 The _____ look so colorful this autumn!
- ○ leaf　　○ leafs
- ○ leafes　○ leaves

10 Some of my favorite _____ are tall tales.
- ○ storys　　○ stories
- ○ storis　　○ story

11 My _____ house is nearby.
- ○ grandparents　○ grandparent's
- ○ grandparents'　○ grandparentes

12 Our family _____ a trip last summer.
- ○ take　　○ takes
- ○ taken　　○ took

GO ON ➡

Language

Mark the answer that is written correctly.

13
- ○ This are my favorite books.
- ○ This is my favorite books.
- ○ These are my favorite books.

14
- ○ Our school starts in September.
- ○ Our school starts in the September.
- ○ Our school starts in the september.

15
- ○ Please pass your sister the salad. He wants it.
- ○ Please pass your sister the salad. She wants it.
- ○ Please pass your sister the salad. She wants them.

16
- ○ You and I play soccer. We are on the same team.
- ○ You and I play soccer. We is on the same team.
- ○ You and I play soccer. They are on the same team.

17
- ○ The dog wants to take a walk. Please get it's leash.
- ○ The dog wants to take a walk. Please get its leash.
- ○ The dog wants to take a walk. Please get their leash.

18
- ○ Nico is the fastest runner.
- ○ Nico is the more faster runner.
- ○ Nico is the most fastest runner.

19
- ○ At the party, there will be a lot of the dancing.
- ○ At the party, there will be a lot of dancing.
- ○ At the party, there will be a lot of dancings.

20
- ○ I will have some milk with my soup.
- ○ I will have some milks with my soup.
- ○ I will have some milks with my soups.

STOP

Mechanics

Read the paragraph. Then read the question about each underlined part and mark your answer. The sample has been done for you.

> **Sample**
>
> Nuts grow in almost every area of <u>the World. Hawaii</u> is famous for macadamia nuts.
>
S
>
> **S** Which shows the correct way to write Part S?
>
> ○ the World Hawaii   ● the world. Hawaii   ○ the world. hawaii   ○ Correct as it is.

The cherry blossom is <u>japans national flower.</u> <u>The people of japan</u> celebrate the return

                                             1   2

of the <u>cherry blossom's each spring</u> with dances and songs. <u>Japanese americans also</u>

                      3   4

celebrate the arrival of <u>the beautiful delicate blossoms.</u> <u>In San francisco California,</u> the

                                      5   6

celebration is held in April. <u>It includes karate dancing and crafts.</u>

                                  7

1 Which shows the correct way to write Part 1?

○ Japans national flower.

○ Japan's national flower.

○ Correct as it is.

2 Which shows the correct way to write Part 2?

○ The People of japan

○ The people of Japan

○ Correct as it is.

3 Which shows the correct way to write Part 3?

○ cherry blossoms each spring

○ cherry blossoms' each spring

○ Correct as it is.

4 Which shows the correct way to write Part 4?

○ japanese Americans also

○ Japanese Americans also

○ Correct as it is.

5 Which shows the correct way to write Part 5?

○ the beautiful, delicate blossoms.

○ the beautiful delicate, blossoms.

○ Correct as it is.

6 Which shows the correct way to write Part 6?

○ In San Francisco California,

○ In San Francisco, California,

○ Correct as it is.

7 Which shows the correct way to write Part 7?

○ It includes karate, dancing, and crafts.

○ It includes, karate, dancing, and crafts.

○ Correct as it is.

GO ON ➡️

Read the letter. Then read the question about each underlined part and mark your answer.

375 Timber Lake Lane

<u>pine grove, Ca 95390</u>
8

July 19, 2002

Dear Ms. Bauers,

I have some exciting <u>news for you There is a piano</u> at the cabin where we are
                                                     9

staying. <u>I have been practiceing</u> a lot every day. <u>Do you know why</u> It's because the weather
                    10   11

has been terrible. <u>By last Saturday I had</u> learned my favorite piece by heart. Please add the
                                   12

<u>Minuet in G</u> by J. S. Bach to the program for the fall concert. <u>I'll be ready to play it!</u>
    13   14

<u>Your student:</u>
        15

Sylvia Lessem

8 Which shows the correct way to write Part 8?

○ Pine grove, Ca 95390

○ Pine Grove, CA 95390

○ Correct as it is.

9 Which shows the correct way to write Part 9?

○ news for you! There is a piano

○ news for you? There is a piano

○ Correct as it is.

10 Which shows the correct way to write Part 10?

○ I have been practice

○ I have been practicing

○ Correct as it is.

11 Which shows the correct way to write Part 11?

○ Do you know why.

○ Do you know why?

○ Correct as it is.

12 Which shows the correct way to write Part 12?

○ By last saturday, i had

○ By last Saturday, I had

○ Correct as it is.

13 Which shows the correct way to write Part 13?

○ "Minuet in G"

○ Minuet in "G"

○ Correct as it is.

14 Which shows the correct way to write Part 14?

○ I'l be ready to play it!

○ Il'l be ready to play it!

○ Correct as it is.

15 Which shows the correct way to write Part 15?

○ Your student.

○ Your student,

○ Correct as it is.

Research Skills

Use the information on the dictionary page to answer each question. Mark your answer.

fortification ➤ foundation

fortification 1. The act of strengthening something: *a wall built as part of the fortification of the town.* 2. Something that strengthens, such as a wall or embankment. **for·ti·fi·ca·tion** (fôr′tə fi kā′shən) *noun, plural* **fortifications.**

fortify 1. To make stronger or more secure: *They fortified the town by building high walls around it* 2. To add strengthening ingredients to: enrich: *This breakfast cereal is fortified with vitamins and iron.* **for·ti·fy** (fôr′tə fī) *verb,* **fortified, fortifying.**

fortress A strong place that can be defended against attack; fort. **for·tress** (fôr′tris) *noun, plural* **fortresses.**

fortunate Having or resulting from good luck; lucky: *One fortunate person has won the contest twice.* **for·tu·nate** (fôr′chə nit) *adjective.*

forwards Another spelling for the adverb forward. **for·wards** (fôr′wərdz) *adverb.*

fossil The hardened remains or traces of an animal or plant that lived long ago: *The fossils we found were imprints of ancient seashells in rock.* **fos·sil** (fos′əl) *noun, plural* **fossils.**

fossil fuel A fuel formed from the remains of prehistoric plants and animals. Coal and petroleum are fossil fuels.

foster To help the growth or development of: *My parents fostered my interest in music. Verb.* ° Giving or receiving care in a family without being related by birth or adoption: *The state has a special department that tries to find foster parents for homeless children. Adjective.* **fos·ter** (fôs′tər) *verb,* **fostered, fostering;** *adjective.*

fought Past tense of fight. **fought** (fôt) *verb.*

1 What will the last entry on this page be?
- ○ forwards
- ○ fought
- ○ foundation

2 Which of these gives correct information about the word *fortification*?
- ○ It is an entry word.
- ○ It is a guide word.
- ○ It is a guide word and an entry word.

3 What part of speech is the word *forwards*?
- ○ adjective
- ○ adverb
- ○ verb

4 If the word *forty* were added to this page, which word would come right before it?
- ○ fortunate
- ○ forwards
- ○ fought

5 Which of these entries does **not** include a sample sentence?
- ○ fortify
- ○ fortunate
- ○ fossil fuel

6 According to the definitions on the dictionary page, which of these is true?
- ○ A fortress is impossible to defend.
- ○ A fortunate person has good luck.
- ○ A fossil is a live plant.

GO ON ➤

Research Skills

Read this encyclopedia article.

422 **Fossil**

© Catherine Ursillo, Photo Researchers

Fossils, such as these dinosaur skeletons, help museum visitors visualize ancient species. Scientists study fossils to learn about the development and ways of life of prehistoric organisms.

Fossil

Fossil is the mark or remains of a plant or animal that lived thousands or millions of years ago. Some fossils are leaves, shells, or skeletons that were preserved after a plant or animal died. Others are tracks or trails left by moving animals.

Most fossils are found in *sedimentary rocks*. These fossils formed from plant or animal remains that were quickly buried in *sediments*—the mud or sand that collects at the bottom of rivers, lakes, swamps, and oceans. After thousands of years, the weight of upper layers of sediment pressing down on the lower layers turned them into rock (see **Sedimentary rock**). A few fossils are whole plants or animals that have been preserved in ice, tar, or hardened sap.

The oldest fossils are microscopic traces of bacteria that scientists believe lived about $3\frac{1}{2}$ billion years ago. The oldest animal fossils are remains of *invertebrates* (animals without a backbone) estimated to be about 700 million years old. The oldest fossils of *vertebrates* (animals with a backbone) are fossil fish about 500 million years old.

Steven M. Stanley, the contributor of this article, is Professor of Earth and Planetary Sciences at The Johns Hopkins University. He has written several books on paleontology.

Fossils are more common and easier to find than many people realize. For example, fossils are plentiful in nearly every state in the United States. Even so, scientists believe that only a small portion of the countless plants and animals that have lived on earth have been preserved as fossils. Many species are thought to have lived and died without leaving any trace whatsoever in the fossil record.

Although the fossil record is incomplete, many important groups of animals and plants have left fossil remains. These fossils help scientists discover what forms of life existed at various periods in the past and how these prehistoric species lived. Fossils also indicate how life on earth has gradually changed over time. This article explains how fossils provide information on ancient life. For a description of animals of the past, see **Prehistoric animal**; for a description of early human beings, see **Prehistoric people**.

How fossils reveal the past

In the distant past, when most fossils formed, the world was different from today. Plants and animals that have long since vanished inhabited the waters and land. A region now covered with high mountains may have been the floor of an ancient sea. Where a lush tropical forest thrived millions of years ago, there may now be a cool, dry plain. Even the continents have drifted far from the positions they occupied hundreds of millions

GO ON ➡

Use the encyclopedia article to answer these questions. Mark your answer. The sample has been done for you.

Sample

Which of these articles would appear in the same volume as "Fossil"?

- ○ Desert
- ● Fish
- ○ Reptiles

1 Which of these is the entry word?
- ○ Dinosaur
- ○ Fossil
- ○ How fossils reveal the past

2 Which of these is <u>not</u> a fossil?
- ○ leaves
- ○ sediment
- ○ shells
- ○ skeletons

3 Which article should you read to find information on early humans?
- ○ Prehistoric animals
- ○ Prehistoric people
- ○ Sedimentary rock

4 Using the information in the text, which of these is true?
- ○ The oldest fossils found are vertebrates.
- ○ The oldest fossils found are microscopic bacteria.
- ○ The oldest fossils found are invertebrates.

Read each of these items about doing research. Mark your answer.

5 What is the first step in the research process?
- ○ locating resources
- ○ deciding what to look up
- ○ choosing a topic
- ○ organizing information

6 Which of these words comes just before **orchestra** in alphabetical order?
- ○ order
- ○ orcus
- ○ orchard
- ○ orchid

7 When you are skimming an article, it is <u>not</u> important to read the
- ○ title
- ○ first two paragraphs
- ○ headings
- ○ ending paragraph

8 When you take notes, it is <u>not</u> important to
- ○ put quotation marks around the words you copy
- ○ put your research question at the top of your card
- ○ write down every word
- ○ write down the source of the information

9 Which of these would you use to find the pages in a book that contain information about your topic?
- ○ copyright page
- ○ index
- ○ glossary
- ○ title page

Name _____ Date _____

Self-Assessment Form

**Look at the writing in your portfolio. Use this form
to help you think about how you're doing as a writer.**

What kinds of writing did you do?

_____

_____

Which piece of writing is your favorite? Why do you like it?

_____

_____

How is your first piece of writing different from your last?

_____

_____

What have you learned about your writing? What do you like to write about?
What kinds of sentences or words do you like to use?

_____

_____

What is hard for you? Mark the things you need to work on.

☐ Choosing the right words   ☐ Organizing ideas before I write

☐ Making my writing clear, organized,   ☐ Finding information and doing
   and interesting   research

☐ Using the English language correctly, especially _____

☐ Other. Explain: _____

_____

What will you do the next time to help you do your best writing?

_____

_____

_____

**Student Self-Assessment
Form**   **16A**   **For the
                                                              Portfolio**